Herron *Notebooks*

Buildings in Japan

Ron Herron
Simon Herron
Andrew Herron

Edited by Sutherland Lyall

Artemis
London Zürich Munich

First published 1993 by
Artemis London Limited

Art direction by
Jonathan Moberly
Designed by
Borja Goyarrola

Imageset by
The Alphabet Set London

Printed in Hong Kong

British Library Cataloguing
in Publication Data
A CIP record for this book
is available from the British
Library

ISBN 1 874056 90 0 (London)
ISBN 3 7608 8403 2 (Zürich)

Artemis London Limited
37 Alfred Place
London WC1E 7DP

Herron
Notebooks

Buildings in Japan

Contents

Toyama prefecture

Toyama is a compact prefecture on the north side of Japan's main island, Honshu. Tokyo is an hour's flight to the south east, Osaka around the same distance to the south west. Toyama's natural boundaries are a crescent of high mountains to the south and east encircling a flood plain around Toyama Bay, which is an arm of the Japan Sea.

Machi no Kao

Over the previous years several Japanese prefectures had commissioned foreign architects for major profile-raising projects, notably the Osaka Expo of 1990 for whose site a mix of Japanese and overseas architects designed a set of follies together with a subsequent project (Nexus World) for a series of buildings in Fukuoka by four European and American architects. There was also the Art Polis project in Kumamoto prefecture: the design of a number of more extensive public and institutional buildings by European and Japanese architects.

Following the proposal for a Japan Expo '92 in Toyama in July 1992, prefectural governor Yukata Nakaoki conceived the idea of a design-seeding project, Machi no Kao, literally The Face of the Town. Inspired by the occasion of the four-month-long expo, it was to be an independent programme of small permanent projects set in the villages and towns of the prefecture. The intention was that the projects should develop from the local culture and traditions of each town – interpreted with a fresh eye by non-Japanese architects of international stature. The projects were to enrich the local culture and visual environment. In addition to their symbolic role, they should become seeds for the future growth of cultural amenities in the locality.

As is usual when major Japanese architectural projects are set up, Arata Isozaki was asked to become commissioner for the project. He is godfather to the most important of the Japanese architectural families, wielding enormous influence in the culture of the country and dispensing patronage throughout his loose network of architects and architectural practices.

He asked his partner Shuichi Fujie to act as producer to develop the project and handle the politics. At the same time he appointed the Workshop for Architecture and Urbanism as enablers and the Urban Factory under the guidance of Shuichi Fujie as design co-ordinators and administrators. The Workshop for Architecture and Urbanism is headed up by Akira Suzuki and Kayoko Ota who are primarily involved in organizing cultural events and publishing the lively architectural magazine Telescope.

Master architect was Tom Heneghan, working for the project as a member of the Urban Factory. A Briton, well known internationally as a winner of competitions, in 1989 he had gone to work in Japan where he found himself immediately absorbed into the Isozaki clan structure and given design commissions including an eleven-building complex for the new Grasslands Institute, part of the Art Polis programme.

His critical role here was to negotiate with those Toyama towns which indicated they wanted to be involved with Machi no Kao, suggest the broad outline of possible projects and, with a committee, select appropriate overseas architects. Then his function, together with the committee of the Urban Factory, effectively became that of client for each of the projects, mediating between the architects, the client mayors and town councils, the local architects and the other professional advisors who were to produce the detail drawings and specifications for construction.

Toyama prefecture was to pay half the construction costs, the local town half, although some of them were later to increase their contributions.

In April 1991 Heneghan and the Urban Factory began the process of sifting through the list of towns, negotiating with them, suggesting more innovative alternatives than the towns had come up with, and finally agreeing 16 schemes. Then over a series of long meetings the committee selected the foreign architects. Because the projects had budgets in the region of only ¥40 million or so (around £150,000), it was decided to offer each architect several projects. The travel budget allowed each of them four or five site visits. The practices chosen in August 1991 were those of Enric Miralles and Cesar Portela from Spain, the London-based Venezuelan Carlos Villenueva-Brandt and Britons Peter Salter, Benson & Forsyth and Herron Associates @ Imagination.

By early October 1991 all the practices had made their first visit to Toyama for initial briefings from their client town councils.

In August Herron Associates, at that time part of the big design firm Imagination (whose London headquarters building they had built), were commissioned to work on projects for Kosugi and Kurobe. In October they were also asked to take on the Daimon project.

Designing by fax

Given their long preoccupation with communications, the Herrons were excited by the prospect of designing by fax. And there was the prospect of passing electronic drawings backwards and forwards by modem. Andrew Herron, a leading-edge Apple Macintosh CAD specialist, had the facilities of Imagination's 30–40 networked Macs and Tom Heneghan in Tokyo had just acquired a Mac. As it turned out, most of the drawings produced by the Herron office were hand-drawn sketches, the only computer images being formal presentation drawings and computer models. The Taiyo Tent engineers naturally designed on computer but it was more convenient for them to fax printed output which could be annotated on the other side of the world and sent back than to send CAD digital files electronically.

Although the Toyama projects might have been technologically very interesting had the Herrons done their drawings directly on the computer and flashed the files backward and forward between Japan and London, that would have called for a special kind of machine, one which allowed Ron Herron to see the line leaving the end of the pen and – unlike current pen-computers – one which left the faintly shaky hand-drawn line unchanged, not digitally tidied up and straightened out. Herron is waiting for that kind of computer package.

More potentially problematic were the cultural differences. In a Toyama seminar on the issue of designing for another country, Herron argued that it was really not all that different from designing a project in, say, the USA.

'OK, the Americans speak English. But you're actually dealing with a different culture even there. And in this case we have been tremendously backed up by Tom Heneghan and Shuichi Fujie and Kasahuro Ando of the Urban Factory who were effectively our clients.

'I imagine that working from the UK by fax directly with a client would be very difficult. Often we weren't aware of the internal stuff that was going on here which they smoothed out for us. We were also very privileged in being set up by them as important designers so that the towns listened to us. It would have been almost impossible in a similar UK town. This culture accepts the poetic bit.'

Herron had also found that he felt a particular affinity with Japanese attitudes.

'Cesar Portela, for example, is trying to tune in to the culture and his architecture is very directly influenced by its architectural traditions. My closeness is with the Japanese comfortableness with the idea of change.'

In the end Herron was convinced that with the same kind of Urban Factory interface it would be possible to carry out large-scale projects by fax because you were carrying out essentially visual conversations.

Naturally there were problems. They were occasionally to do with missed deadlines for which in one or two cases the local architects covered, anxious not to show the famous foreign architect in a bad light to the Town Council. In other cases urgent decisions were innocently made in Japan which the London office thought were against the spirit of the design. It is not easy to convey the unique design culture of an office via fax.

Face-to-face meetings in Japan were essential. They were partly an opportunity for Herron to meet old Japanese friends (he had taught with Isozaki at UCLA in the late 1960s and had met many of the luminaries as over the years they passed and re-passed through London and the Architectural Association), to give lectures and seminars and meet with local architects – and members of the local town communities. But their primary importance was in working with Heneghan and Ando, together with the local architects and engineers, in establishing the fine detail of form and structure, sometimes in very extended sessions.

So communications were by fax and meetings. Designing was done in the usual Herron way, Rotring pen sketches drawn straight out of Ron Herron's head in clear line without any of the tentative, heavily revised scratching you see crumpled up in most architects' dustbins. Of course there are revisions, but they are almost always revisions of the whole form or the whole detail. He thinks in his head and gets it down as quickly as possible, rather than thinking on paper.

In the Herron office, schemes tend to kick off with Ron because, as Andrew Herron put it, 'He just gets into it. Simon and I aren't as good at making that quick decision which makes it all start. Simon will make 58 versions so he can make a selection. In a way he likes the process of not deciding, he likes to explore the idea – and he hates it when he finds the design has already been decided. Particularly in the Toyama project this was a major point of friction.'

Ron Herron defends himself on the grounds that there isn't always a great enough flow of work to be able to allocate it and that anyway he is impatient. To the outside observer it appears that he is not particularly interested in the process. He likes putting the idea down, maybe after mulling it over in the car or thinking in the abstract over a period of months.

'What enables you to make fast decisions is that you've worked it out without knowing and here is an opportunity to use it. An idea gets gradually refined, reassessed, and suddenly you see a way of applying it. I'm dying to capture it on paper. You worry about not getting the idea down.'

The Toyama projects were designed by a loose group in the Herron Associates @ Imagination office: Ron in his customary role of atelier master, Simon and James Philipps more or less running detail design, James for a time and then Simon as the communications channel via fax with Tom Heneghan of the Urban Factory. Andrew Herron was also involved in the design conversations and from time to time other people, such as Anthony Leung, Towon Sin Gan and Ariff A. Nik, working on concurrent projects, participated, mainly creating computer drawings and images.

Kosugi

Kosugi is a small market town on a very flat site. There is light industry and housing to the south of the railway line and the old town to the north. The train station has the usual simple linear canopy over the island platform with an underpass leading south from the station forecourt to a newer plaza, north to the old. Visitors to the Japan Expo '92 were to be bussed from there to the expo site some kilometres away. The brief was to design a memorable canopy for waiting expo shuttle-bus passengers and new public toilets to the west of the underpass staircase.

Briefing: August 1991

In late August 1991 on his first visit to Toyama, Ron Herron met the mayor of Kosugi, Kazuo Mikami, and the town council. They discussed the details of the brief and the deadline: the end of June when the Toyama Expo commenced. With construction starting in March, three months were needed for the local executive architects, Yazuhiro Fukumi and Shigeaki Doda of the Fukumi Sekkei practice, to prepare the formal contract drawings. That meant the design had to be fixed by the end of November when Herron was scheduled to make his next visit to Japan.

Sitting listening at the Kosugi briefing with Tom Heneghan and Kazuhiro Ando, Herron made sketch notes of the plan of the station and its forecourt and squiggled the outline of a fabric canopy across the forecourt, partly covering the new toilets to the left, and indicated a recladdding to the concrete safety walls of the subway ramp. His preliminary notion was to use modular French lavatories of the kind which had been installed around central London – here wrapped with a metal mesh – perhaps a reference to old Parisian pissoirs, certainly a continuation of the long Herron pre-occupation with wrapping.

toilets – packaged →
+ wrapped.
under canopy

First sketch proposals: September 1991

Back in London, Ron Herron talked through the brief with Simon Herron and James Philipps. They set to work on exploring the possibilities, notably that of an all-glass canopy with a big information board. Time was very short and there were some early tensions – as they discussed it later:

Simon: On Canada Water [the Jubilee Line London Underground station project on which they had recently been working] we had been exploring the idea of a bus waiting area as an egg-crate structure in a series of layers and we thought here that we could extend the idea as a linear grid.

Ron: I thought this was wrong. The glass plus egg crate was right for an urban London context which worked well against the plastic forms of the entrance: a very cool roof with a very nice tension between the two.

Here I think if you had put in a supercool thing it would have disappeared against the jumble of the station. What it needed was expressiveness. It's the gateway to an expo, you need something carefree – and something fruity like the free-form toilets.

After some argument, we went back to the fabric idea. In a normal project we would probably have followed through this and other ideas. But this design programme was superfast – just two weeks. We couldn't hang about. Really we were borrowing something from our own back pocket, our own design history, things like the Imagination Building roof [whose fabric roof cost a third of an early glass proposal] and a whole series of earlier fabric projects.

So I made the decision that we should give them the biggest canopy we could afford and that it should be colourful and have a dynamic which we could achieve more easily than with glass.

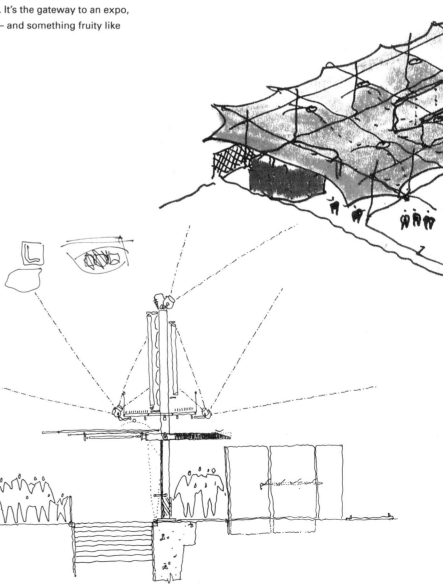

The idea Ron Herron had been sketching out at the same time as the glass proposals was a development of his first drawing from the Toyama meeting. It turned into a bright red two-hump-wide canopy across the front of the station using much the same structural arrangement as that used in the Imagination Building atrium roof. A mesh screen half shielded the utilitarian station structures at the rear, and the lavatory block, still a vague free-form shape, was located to the right. Tall hanging banners lined the two adjacent sides of the square. These were the preliminary sketch design ideas they sent on 13 September to Tom Heneghan at the Urban Factory for him to show Kosugi Town Council – together with a deliberately poetic description (which produced some difficulties for the translators in Tokyo – particularly the final sentence).

THE PINK CLOUD

Our proposal aims to generate a landmark not only in the physical sense but also to serve as a symbol of Kosugi's commitment to search for and explore contemporary form. Our proposal relates contextual opportunities and the specificity of place with the technical, functional and programmatic requirements. We believe in an architecture which is carefully deployed as a means of giving pleasure and delight.

Both structure and fabric were conceived in the spirit of growth and change, of flexibility, responsiveness and indeterminacy, of celebrating the dimension of time in architecture and allowing for and encouraging future development. Here it is a language of canopies and screens, a vocabulary of shade, shadow and light, a series of carefully considered interventions echoing the ambiguity of festival space, gaining its pleasure from the incomplete.

The first manoeuvre is to deploy a single continuous canopy which defines territory and provides shelter. The roof floats effortlessly, gently articulated, maintaining an air of detachment from its surroundings, the tracery network of the supporting structure merging into the background of the town. Beneath the canopy, the new block of toilets, a series of screens and the exit from the underpass all exist as independent elements. The use of bright and vivid colours in broad planes of colour takes reference from contemporary Japanese poster illustration.

This proposal exists in isolation from the broad context of the immediate area. We must at some time look at the whole: the issue of a town divided, the relationship between north and south station plazas and their relationship with the station considered as a single point along a communications and temporal line.

Development of the idea: October 1991

To Simon Herron and Ron Herron
From Kayoko Ota, Workshop for Architecture and
Urbanism
2 October 1991

Dear Ron and Simon
I am sending you herewith the Town's questions to you and
comments by Suichi Fujie of Urban Factory concerning
your proposals submitted in September.

Questions from Kosugi Town
1   Canopy covered with fabric tent
1.1 The proposal seems to give too strong an impression as
     a temporary structure although it is expected to be a
     permanent one.
1.2 Will fabric sheet be strong enough to bear the load of
     snow and rainwater? Won't it wear considerably in due
     course?
1.3 Won't partitioning across the front make a tight or
     squeezy feeling in space. Won't it make people feel
     uneasy because it will shutter their view? Will it be
     suitable for a place to accommodate a lot of people?
2   Toilets
     How are the location, form and structure of toilets
     considered so far? How would you relate them to the
     canopy proposed?
3   Entrance to underpass and walkway pavement
     What are your views as to the redesign of the entrance
     cover to underpass and the widening of the walkway
     pavement?
4   Colour
     The Town wants options for the main colour. Can you
     propose others?

Comments by Shuichi Fujie, Urban Factory
     The tent and canopy as well as banners and flags will
     give an impression of festive occasion and of
     temporariness. Would you also like to consider the
     possibility of the following:
     for the tent to cover only part of the plaza rather than
     the entire plaza
     for part of the tent to be removed and for the frames
     to be exposed after the expo is over
     for the frame to be made of concrete, for example,
     rather than steel which may appear too temporary?
We would also have to make sure of the feasibility of the
materials.

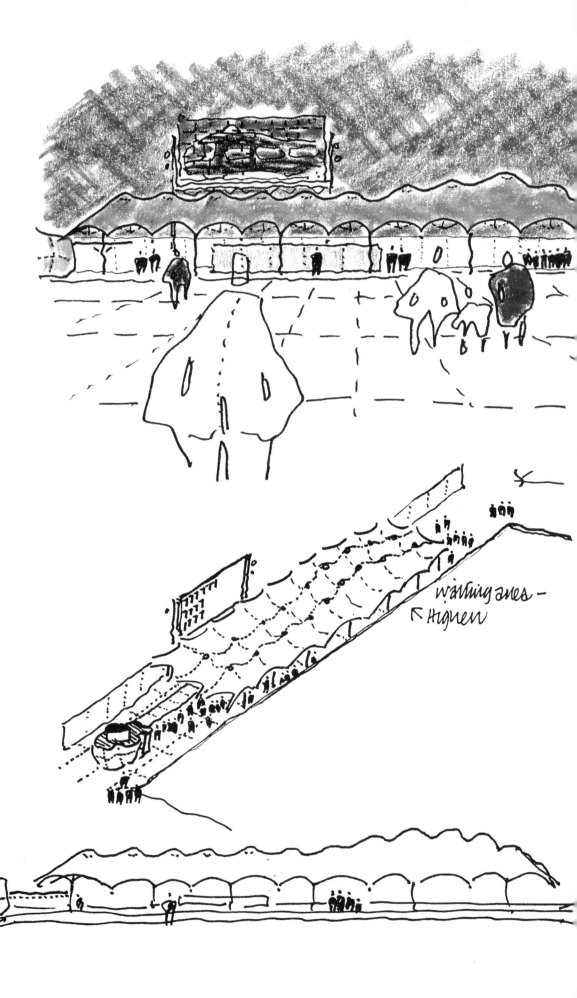

Unfazed by these preliminary reactions to the September ideas sketches (mainly to do with worries about the perceived ephemeral quality of the canopy), the Herrons continued working up the basic fabric idea. They were relying partly on their clients gradually getting used to the idea and partly on Tom Heneghan explaining it and smoothing their uncertainties.

At this stage in late October, cost studies in Japan indicated that the area of fabric would have to be reduced. So the Herrons rethought the canopy's extent and form. Keeping the double row of support columns, they shortened the canopy, connecting the now-exposed sculptural toilet block with a flat glass strip roof. Playing around with the form of the canopy, they decided to increase its height over the main passenger waiting area.

Although they had abandoned the idea of a glass and egg-crate roof, the big electronic billboard which had formed an integral part of it continued to look like a good idea and was to form an element in the formal presentation by Ron Herron to the Kosugi town council in mid November 1991.

The Herrons realized that the billboard would not come under the budget but suggested to the municipality that here was an ideal opportunity for commercial sponsorship, providing the town with a permanent signpost.

During this time the Urban Factory faxed data about bus turning circles, confirmation of the construction budgets at ¥37 million for the canopy, ¥30 million for the toilets and snow-melting equipment. The catch here was that the structure would have to be designed to carry the full snow loads in case the equipment (electric panels, warm-air ducting or water sprays) failed.

First formal presentation: November 1991

On his second site trip to Japan, between 9 and 16 November, Ron Herron took to Kosugi the formal presentation drawings, a sheet outlining how the design had developed, a small model and a computer model of the Pink Cloud.

    The site plan showed a similar canopy on the other side of the station and an indication of a much more comprehensive urban plan for the whole area; currently the railway line divides the town in two.

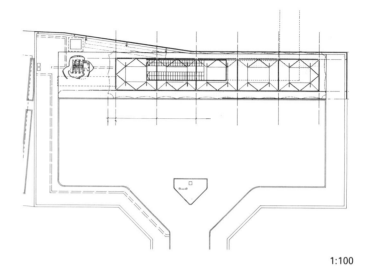

1:100

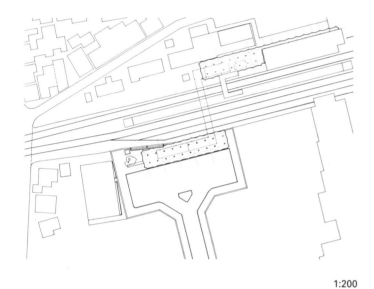

1:200

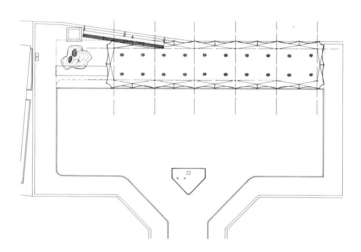

1:100

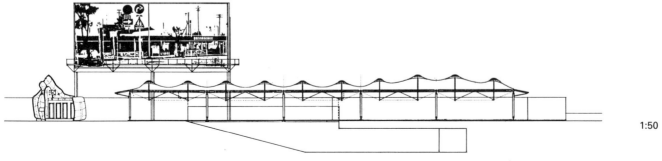

1:50

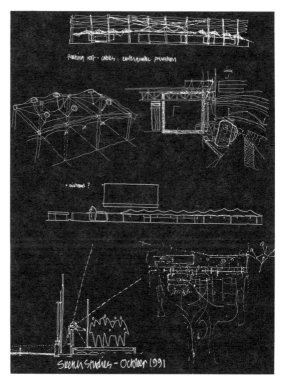

Sketch studies – October 1991

From the beginning it was clear that the whole area of the station, its square, adjoining areas and the other side of the station were in need of an integrated planning exercise. We showed the clients the possibilities as part of our specific design although we recognized that they were not part of the brief.

You always bear in mind that this kind of thing won't be accepted. It's the optional extra which makes the whole design more than just a bit better. But you design so that if it doesn't happen the basic idea still stands on its own.

We are very familiar with the use of fabrics and in a way that was an argument for not using them. But that's what I did in the first bit of thinking. Although Simon and James said 'Why fabric?', I thought we should push for a lighter, cat's cradle like, minimal structure which would take the possibilities of the lightweight roof as far as it could go.

You never go entirely with the first idea because as you design you learn more about the whole thing. What we wanted was a cable-and-strut structure with no compression members meeting; in the end this stick-and-cable structure ended up a bit like a tensegrity structure.

This is the first time in many years that we've found ourselves designing in concrete. The Daimon project is in concrete too but there it had to be because we were building party walls. The obvious thing is to say it's Ando. But really it's to do with Corb. Back in the 1950s we were seen as Brutalists. Now we are seen as high-technology people. I don't see it that way: it's more to do with paring away – more a clean Brutalism, more reductive. I take tough surfaces as being fundamentally enjoyable: I've always had problems with marble floors, for example.

Here we had low budgets so we have off-the-form concrete and granolithic floors. Even the benches for the handbasins are concrete, polished and lacquered. You could say the form is Miesian but the detailing and finishes are not. They are Brutal in, I suppose, the sense of Hunstanton. The glass blocks are probably a reference to Corb at the Clarté apartment building in Geneva.

The mesh also appears at Daimon, here less than we had originally intended. We've always been interested in the idea of wrapping – not just the Christo bit, which I've always admired, but also in a number of Archigram projects in the 1960s. Somebody suggested that we've been looking at Gehry who has made mesh part of the current architectural conversation, but for me it's an affectionate memory of the big mesh wall surrounding the rooftop recreation space at Brixton School of Building in the 1940s.

Why pink? I had always drawn Kosugi with a red/pink canopy. It started as red and it got pinker and hotter. We talked about using red – and there was difficulty in getting the fabric in anything other than crude standard colours. But I said 'Sod it, let's do what we draw for a change' – and the Taiyo Tent people came up with exactly the right colour at a standard price.

The site was scruffy, cables, frantic, really messy townscape – like a Gordon Cullen before sketch. Because we could touch only certain things in that environment – and couldn't tidy up any of that stuff, we needed a powerful image. My view was that the only thing to do was not be polite.

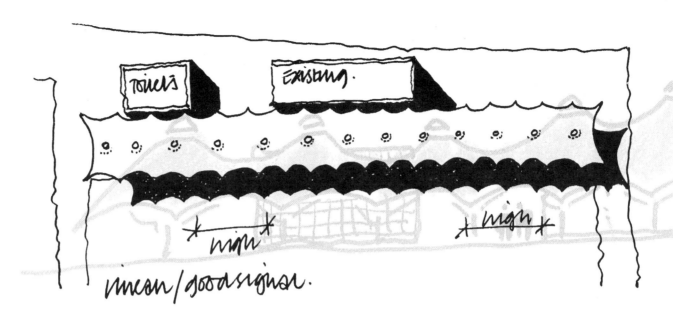

In Japan: November 1991

During his meeting with the local executive architectural practice Fukumi Sekkei, Ron Herron talked through a variety of ideas (summarized on the facing page), a number of them to do with the surroundings – replacing the existing safety enclosure around the subway ramp, adding glass wind screens to the front and rear of the waiting area, wrapping a proposed pump room with mesh and running a mesh screen around the back of the site, partly to enclose it and partly to screen out much of the tatty view.

Back in London at the end of November Tom Heneghan broke the news that the canopy and its structure were going to cost twice the budget figure.

From Tom Heneghan
To Ron Herron
29 November 1991

We met yesterday to try to calculate some more cost guidelines for you and have consulted today with a fabric roof contractor to get a rough price for the Kosugi roof.

The budget is a great problem. We have received from a specialist company a very rough estimate of ¥80 million for the fabric roof including the steel structure but excluding foundations, glass screens, etc.

The price for PVC is ¥40,000 per square metre. It is available in only 11 standard colours – we will receive samples tomorrow.

These figures are very quick estimates.

We would like to suggest a few possibilities which could be adopted in combination:

(a) Perhaps the toilets should be made as simple as possible with a basic construction method so that the maximum amount of money can be transferred to the canopy. Stainless steel is relatively expensive so perhaps the stainless-steel external structure could be changed to (for example) sprayed concrete or ordinary concrete, etc., while the interior remains stainless-steel fittings.

(b) Since the length of the canopy is most important in the composition, perhaps the width could be generally reduced, while the length might be reduced a little.

(c) Perhaps the material can be changed. If vinyl is used instead of PVC the estimate for the whole roof is ¥60 million including steel and erection but excluding foundations. Vinyl will support 400 kg per square metre.

(d) It may be possible to negotiate the transfer of some part of the paving budget to the roof budget so it would be good to consider a minimal paving plan.

James Philipps responded the same day.

We showed your figures to our friendly QS who had a few thoughts: your ¥80,000 per square metre for fabric, cables, etc., seems high (about £360 per square metre) Over here the figure is nearer £260 per square metre.

We are assuming that where you say PVC you mean Teflon. Also our QS chaps feel that ¥20 million for fixing is high – even including the Herron factor.

From your figures we are guessing that they were derived from our earlier presentation drawings and do not take into account the revised grid layout. It is smaller and will make some sort of saving – but probably not enough.

Your idea of a spray concrete construction to the WCs at Kosugi is interesting – is it expensive and can a double curvature be achieved? We are also looking at an option using glass blocks which we feel could be equally successful.

Rumour has it that we are appearing with you in <u>AA Files</u> …

○ ○ vending mach
- suggest position

○ ○ move the two
telephones to under
canopy - no box.

○ ○ seats / say for 10.

① maybe reduce length of canopy to save + to allow some
glass screening.

② structure — to allow snow loading
(1 metre thick) and at same time
earthquake !!
earthquake code for Japan??
will report back to us.

Talk to
Brian.
on la[?]

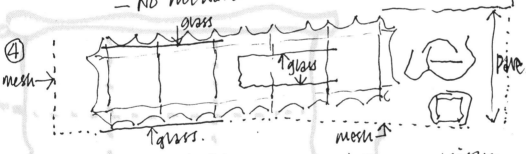

- paint out dark
grey)

← possibly
wrap pump
room / metal
perforated.

③ toilets — no tanks (direct from mains.
— no H.W.P. (direct from mains)
— no hot water.

④

glass

↑ glass

mesh →

↑ glass.

mesh ↑

pave.

⑤ look at making glass screen to ramp higher — so that
snow can't blow in — maybe 2.5 m?

⑥ a) send drwgs. end of NOV. (to umban factory to distribute).
b) next visit (to discuss with LA.) → 15 JAN.

⑦ put light on toilet block for external lighting
to replace tasty street light

⑧ pump room →
DOOR →
window
railway.

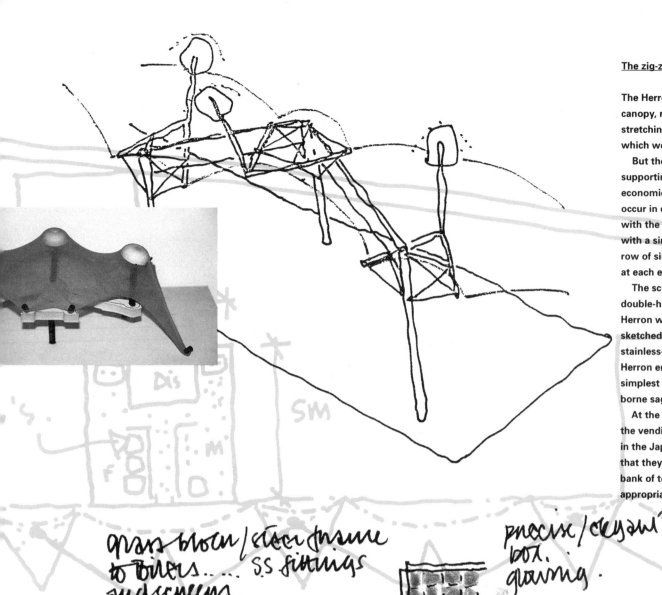

The zig-zag: November 1991

The Herrons had changed the shape and position of the canopy, now much narrower and longer, once again stretching right across the site in front of the toilets which were now lined up with the subway exit.

But the problem remained of how to devise a supporting structure which was both elegant and economical. In one of those pleasing moments which occur in collaborative design, James Philipps came up with the idea of substituting the two rows of columns with a single zig-zag row of posts producing a staggered row of single humps with the whole structure tied down at each end by cables.

The sculptural toilets had been a nice idea but, like the double-hump canopy, they were way over budget. So Herron went entirely in the opposite direction and sketched out a very simple glass-brick box with stainless-steel fittings and internal partitions. From the Herron end it looked very straightforward. Later this simplest of propositions was to develop into a small fax-borne saga of misunderstanding.

At the same time the Herron office asked for images of the vending machines which are to be seen everywhere in the Japanese townscape. Since it seemed inevitable that they would be installed afterwards, together with a bank of telephones, it made sense at least to design appropriate locations for them.

grass block / steel frame
to toilets..... s.s fittings
and screens.

precise / elegant
box.
glazing.

savings !!

≃70m

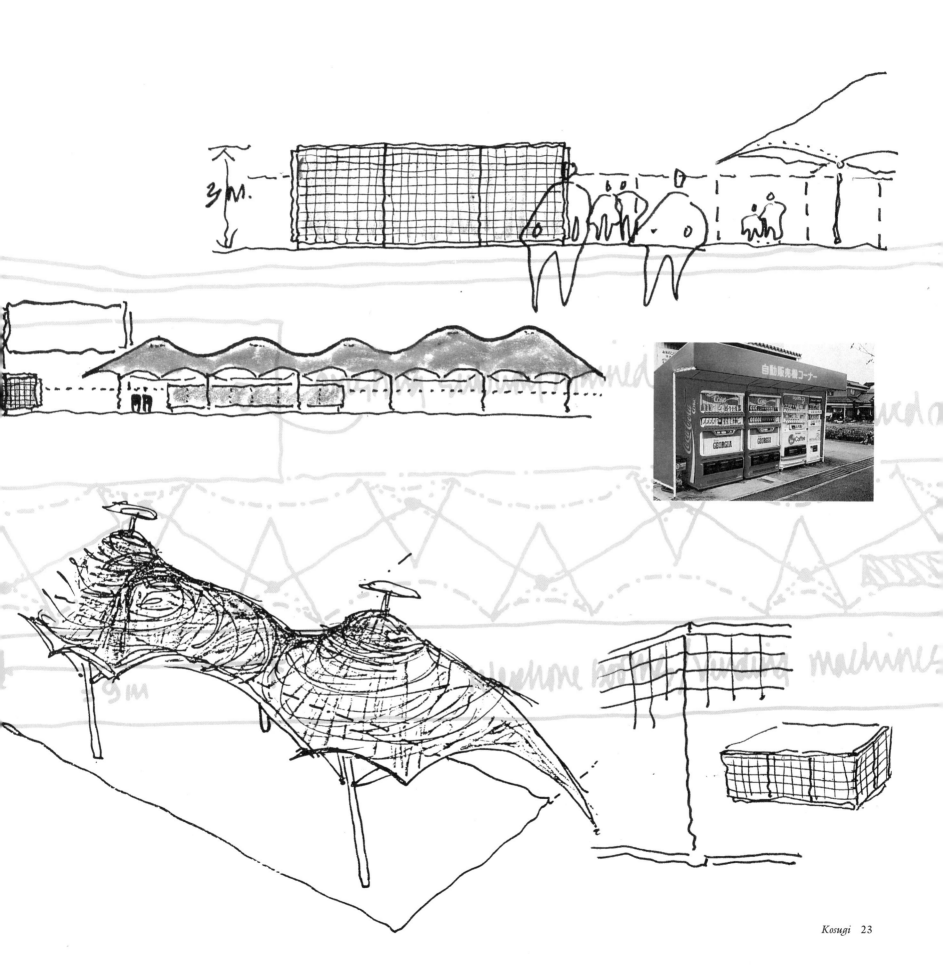

3M.

自動販売機コーナー

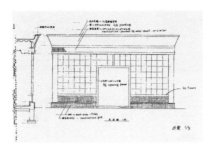
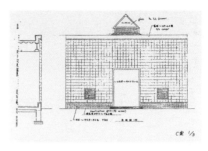

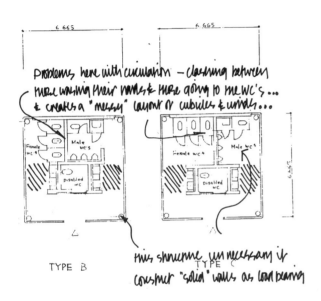

TYPE B

Problems here with circulation — clashing between those washing their hands & those going to the WC's… & creates a "messy" layout of cubicles & urinals…

this showerone unnecessary if construct "solid" walls as load bearing

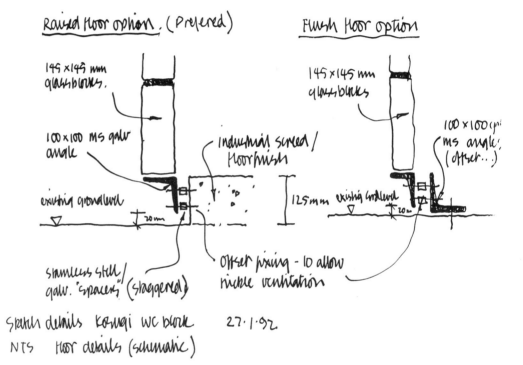

Raised floor option. (Prefered)

Flush floor option

145 × 145 mm glassblocks.

145 × 145 mm glassblocks

100 × 100 MS galv angle

industrial screed / floorfinish

100 × 100 (m) ms angle. (offset…)

existing groundlevel

125 mm existing groundlevel

stainless steel / galv. "spacers" (staggered)

offset fixing - to allow niche ventilation

Sketch details Kosugi WC block   27·1·92
NTS   floor details (schematic)

The toilets: January 1992

One part of the Kosugi project served as a reminder that designing architecture by fax between different countries is not straightforward.

After reworking the toilet block in December, the Herrons had assumed that there was only one way to design a Miesian block. Then the Urban Factory sent a set of alternatives from the local executive architects. Their concern was that the columns would have to support the roof load over the whole 6.7-metre width of the block – and would be bigger than the thickness of the glass blocks.

A few days later Kazuhiro Ando sent three complete exterior redesigns by the local architects for the Herrons to select one (top row, above). The local architects had found the Herron design to be over budget and sent additional plan alternatives.

More than a little bemused at the elevations (there had been a lot of stamping around in the office) James Philipps sent a carefully worded fax.

To Tom Heneghan
From James Philipps
28 January 1992

We are a little concerned that the drawings we are receiving relating to the WCs do not reflect our original design intentions. It appears from the drawings that a very traditional form of construction is being used as the basis for the WC block. This is unnecessary over-complication of what is a modest structure … To keep the costs to a minimum we are treating the block as a simple concrete (cast <u>in situ</u>) roof slab supported on load-bearing concrete internal walls with a glass-block wrap enclosing the space.

We feel that our original layout is still the most efficient use of space defining and separating the WC and washbasin areas, preventing the passing of those washing their hands by those going to the WC cubicles/urinals.

We are unsure that the concrete north wall idea is such a good one – but can see the reasoning for it. It disrupts the original thought of a single jewel set within the present urban environment …

Philipps sent details of the re-entrant corners (the roof was supported by the internal walls in an arguably non-Miesian fashion), a commentary on the plan proposals, and the Herron version (above and facing page).

In fact, the Japanese drawings had been done to meet a deadline set by the Town Council. The Kosugi practice was far too polite to hassle the Herrons for drawings. In turn the Herron office, assuming that a Miesian solution could only be done one way, had not realized that detailed drawings were necessary.

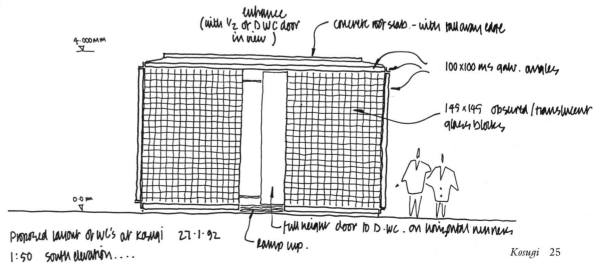

Final design: Christmas 1991

On 17 December the Herron office sent the formal version of the zig-zag design with a model to Japan. In this scheme, the profile of the canopy had acquired several undulations which were reflected in plan by a widening of the canopy edges. The main columns were linked together at their tops by ladder beams and the umbrella push-up struts were supported at the junction of V frames flying on cables attached to the columns. The lateral stability of the structure was achieved by taking the extreme ends of the fabric down to anchor points at ground level.

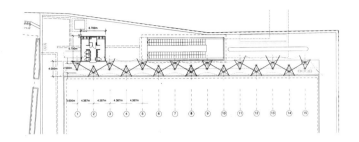

1:1000

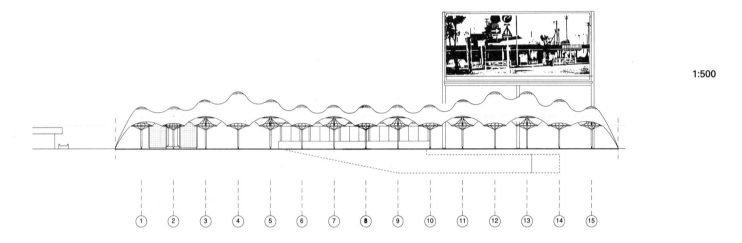

1:500

On 29 December Kazuhiro Ando wrote to Ron Herron, now elevated from Ron-san to Ron-sama.

Thank you very much for sending your beautiful drawings and models ... it was a pleasure to carry them to Toyama and see the grateful faces of the Town people and to hear them speaking highly of them.

And then we had a meeting with the Kosugi people ... this meeting was agreeable and supportive of your new thoughts.

In response to Ando's request for further details of the canopy structure, Simon Herron sent him a sketch section in which the whole canopy was raised to allow buses to park under its edge.

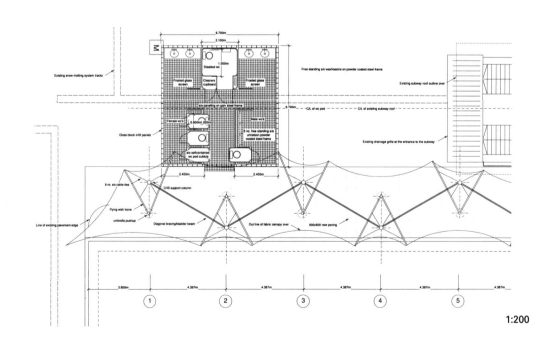

1:200

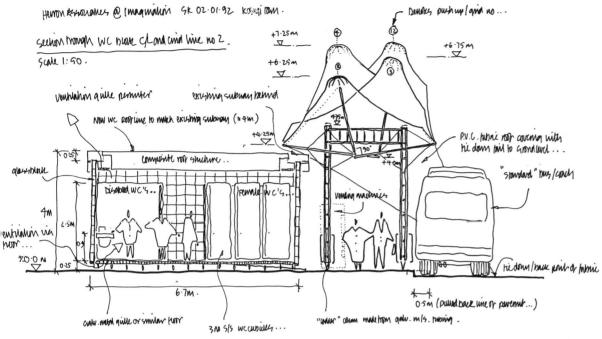

Herron Associates @ Imagination GK 02·01·92 Kosugi Tom.

Section through WC block c/L and cind line no 2
Scale 1:50.

— Denotes push up/grid no...

+7·25m
+6·75m
+6·25m
+4·25m
+4·0m

ventilation grille perimeter — existing subway behind —

New WC roofline to match existing subway (±4m)

P.V.C. fabric roof covering with tie down rail to Ground level...

glass rooflight

Composite roof structure...

4m

Disabled WC's...   Female WC'S...

"standard" bus/coach

vending machines

ventilation via riser...

400M

0·25

0·25

6·7m

0·5m (pulled back line of pavement...)

tie down/back point of fabric

cast metal grille or similar floor

3 No S/S wc cubicles...

"ladder" column made from galv. m/s. tubing.

N.B. i C/L of WC aligns with C/L of subway canopy enclosure... ii height of fabric raised to allow access of expo buses under fabric...

Taiyo were also worried about the smallness of the radius of the umbrellas: they were not sure that the fabric could cope satisfactorily. Finally they were worried about drunks and children climbing up the tie-downs at each end of the canopy.

The Herrons were not happy about the rigid V-frame connections but in principle were happy about cantilevered columns, had half anticipated the problem about drunks and children climbing the tie-down, and thought the idea of anti-rotational cables great: 'They add to the cat's-cradle effect!' wrote James Philipps.

The canopy still exceeded the budget.

In a 22 January fax, Tom Heneghan suggested altering the cutting lines so that they were parallel rather than radiating from the centres of the umbrellas. There was also a probable need to move the canopy along a bit so that people coming up from the subway could walk under cover at a point where there was no column.

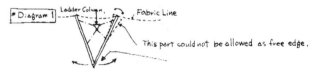

Diagram 1   Ladder Column   Fabric Line

This part could not be allowed as free edge.

Heneghan's fax concluded: 'On a happier note, the Tent Co is negotiating with a supplier to purchase the original special colour at the same cost as standard fabric … The Tent Co expect to take 20 days on site.'

At the end of the first week in January, the Taiyo Tent engineers outlined their preliminary reactions. First, the zig-zag ladder trusses connecting the tops of the columns should be triangulated by adding another member between every second column head in the zig zag. The alternative was to make the columns vertical cantilevers. In addition, their early view was that two of the cables supporting the flying V frame would have to be solid compression struts. Japanese structural regulations would not allow the fabric to be used as part of the structural system.

Further, because the V frames did not seem to have any rotational restraint, there was need for additional cables from their corners to an adjacent column. And bracing would have to be added to the umbrellas to hold them in place. (The Imagination Building umbrellas are held in place by the tension of the fabric over them.)

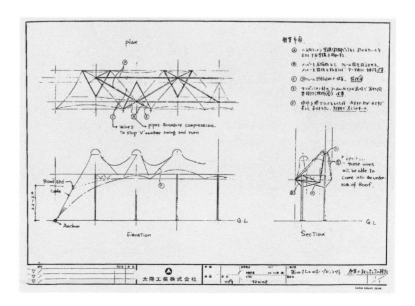

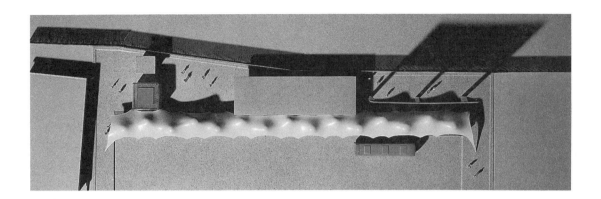

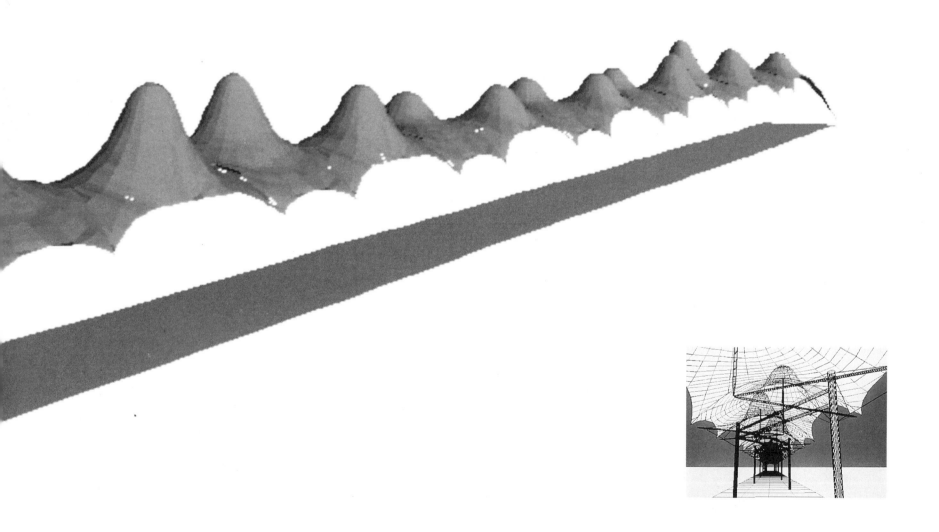

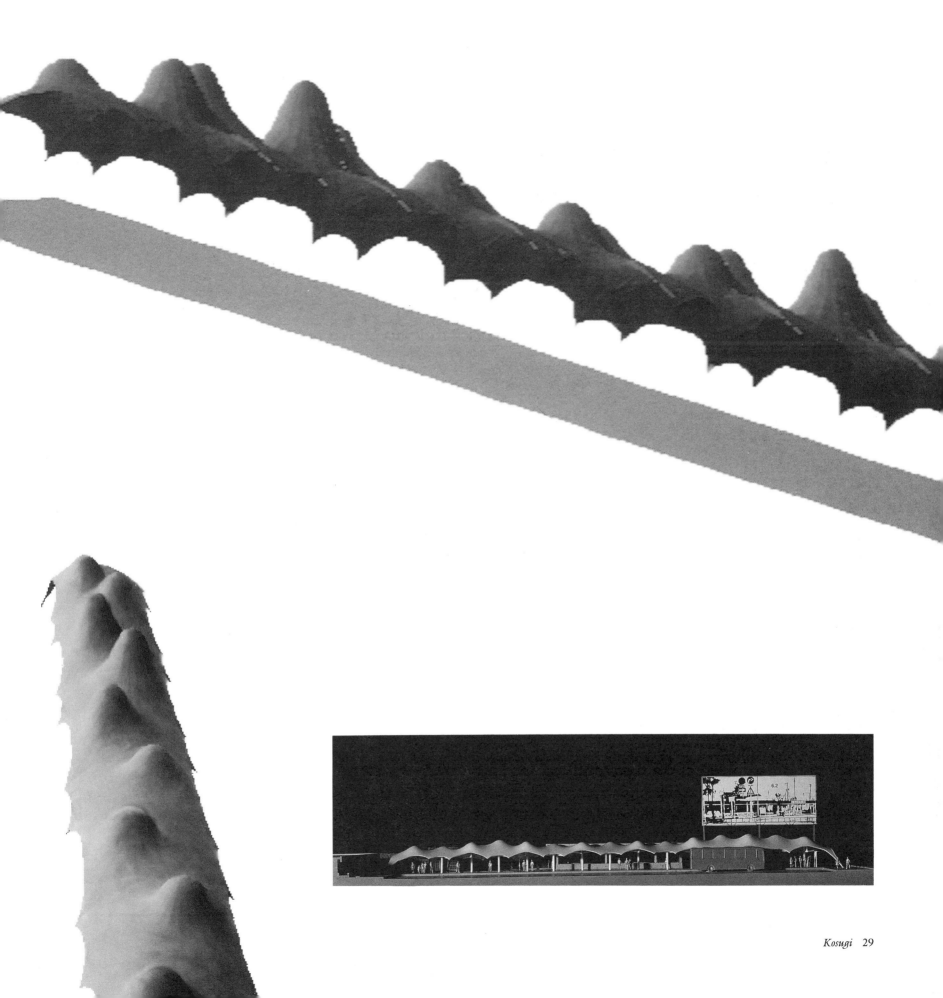

Site visit: January–February 1992

In late January the Herron office in London were rethinking the tie-downs at each end just as Ron Herron was arriving in Japan for a further presentation of the scheme. This included a computer model.

He met with the local executive architects to sort out the toilet block problem face to face and sketched out exactly how to do the Miesian detailing: glass blocks for the walls set in steel frames with simple re-entrant corners, which Heneghan and Ando continues to discuss with the local architects in a dingy coffee bar at Haneda Airport. Later, in his hotel room Herron roughed out the final plan. There had been a discussion about whether this was really Miesian or Brutalist. Herron took the position that the structure and detailing was too crude to be Miesian – rather more Smithsonian Brutalist, à la Hunstanton School. Having established that this was to do with raw surfaces and simply exposed servicing, he confused everybody by announcing that he wanted the ceilings to be painted blue.

The mayor, Kazuo Mikami, is a charming guy. We had designed the toilets as a Brutal grey concrete and glass block and his officials had started to raise the possibility of tiling the walls and floor and using stainless steel. We had had to reject stainless-steel cubicles a long time before on cost grounds. Suddenly Ando-san interrupted sternly in Japanese and when he finished they didn't ask any more questions. That evening two of the officials came up and apologized. I didn't know what for until Ando-san told me what he had said – that Mr. Herron was a famous architect and it was very rude to question his design.

Next day (3 February) was the meeting with Taiyo Tent. They fielded six engineers. They are smashing people and very good.

We had been talking together via fax before and they had now got to a position on the engineering where they wanted to put in more compression members. I wasn't too happy about this and said I don't want two rigid members to meet anywhere. This engineer was smiling politely but you could see that inside he was tearing his hair out. Ando-san said in English that they were deeply worried that they might disappoint me. I said to them 'Try as hard as you can.'

They did. One of the structural problems – apart from earthquakes, which Herron had experienced the day before when a 5.6 Richter earthquake hit his hotel in Tokyo – was the need to design for very high snow loads. The canopies had been redesigned with reasonably steeply sloped peaks but by increasing their height further and achieving angles of more than 50 degrees to throw off the snow, the mandatory design loads could be reduced to zero.

In addition to their computer models, the Taiyo Tent engineers made a 50:1 physical structural model of a bay of the station canopy, and a rough model. They all spent time playing around with the fabric to see how it could be distorted before making a final decision to maintain a continuous height, rather than raising two sections – with the trade-off that the canopy would be widened at these points instead. Herron liked Taiyo's models so much that he asked if he could have them when they were finished with them.

A couple of days of fast computer work later, the Taiyo Tent engineers came back to Herron and said they thought they had cracked it. Five models of the structure were made: the Herrons' and Taiyo Tent's separate computer models, Taiyo Tent's and the Herrons' rough models and the Taiyo Tent structural model.

Structure: February–March 1992

Following Ron Herron's February visit, the final structural details were sorted out by fax. Tom Heneghan annotated the Taiyo Tent drawings (like engineering drawings all over the world, rather enigmatic), faxed them to London where they were either agreed or annotated by Herron and returned. The support structure, designed for robust outdoor public use – and for earthquakes – was now quite different from the delicate Herron/Buro Happold-designed Imagination Building canopy. The basic principle remained: push-ups with umbrella heads supported on an array of tension members. But when it became impossible to brace the structure diagonally with tie-downs, the columns changed from simple vertical supports in axial compression to take on the additional role of vertical cantilevers.

There had been a slight running worry on both sides of the world that everything looked over-dimensioned. The Taiyo engineers worked hard on reducing tube diameters and Heneghan sent a detailed list of their final efforts. Ron Herron was not unhappy about them because if the structure had been pared back to its simplest and most efficient, that was the way it should look.

There had been some unhappiness about the external crease marks on the London building and new umbrellas were devised to provide a smoother, more spherical support – a bit like a crinoline frame – with safety cables to keep them in position and without the turnbuckles of the Imagination Building prototype. Ron Herron was a bit worried that this detail was over-engineered but there it was.

To James Philipps
From Tom Heneghan
20 February 1992

First the unimportant news. The Toyama newspaper has apparently done a big splurge on RH with the computer perspectives in full colour. I'm told it is excellent and we will send you a copy when we can.

Ando and I have just returned from a meeting with Taiyo Tent. It seems that the engineers dealing with the Kosugi structure are so much in love with it that they have been fighting with their computer to get results you will approve of. I don't know how much they brutalized the poor computer, but they have got the sizes down and THE V-FRAME IS NOW HELD ONLY BY TENSION MEMBERS!

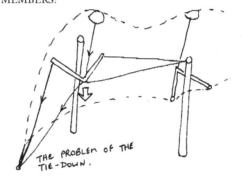

THE PROBLEM OF THE TIE-DOWN.

Now the blotch is the end tie-downs. It is impossible to make them work. In order to stop the V frames rotating, they are to be connected by cables to other column heads and the cables were finally to go to the end tied-down point. But connecting the cables to the tie-downs actually pulls down the point of the V which is being pushed down anyway by the umbrella … Taiyo can make the whole thing 'delicate' if you will accept that the tent ends in columns so that the structural system of each bay continues unchanged to the end of the canopy. (This is a totally different issue from the discussion we had with Ron about people climbing the tie-down cables.)

There's a second blotch. The cables connect to the columns with the usual ears but they need to have collars around the columns to prevent distortion … They will try to get rid of the collars but they are not optimistic.

Taiyo urgently need your approvals for everything – they expect to start fabrication immediately. If possible please reply by our Thursday.

Nothing will be in stainless steel (cost) so everything must be painted. I believe you said it should be white, but could you please send a colour sample – there are so many whites. Japan does not have the same colour system as the UK so a colour number will be no good.

On 21 March, Tom Heneghan faxed the formal Taiyo Tent drawings for general approval by the Herrons: they were to form part of the acceptance drawings in the contract between the Urban Factory and the town so that stage payments could be authorized.

It is a statement of the architect's intention at the completion of Preliminary Design stage … I would like to send you the tent detail drawings but Taiyo are up to their eyeballs making the submission for Building Control and are making a 'perfect' drawing presentation to be sent to you ASAP. I tried to explain that you just needed sketches but I'm afraid the aura of RH has rather got to them and they are unhappy about sending unfinished sketches … They will be perfectly happy to make changes to the 'perfect' set as you wish within the restrictions that detailing in general in Japan is often not as lovely as it can be in the UK and also within the restrictions that Taiyo are already losing their shirt, trousers, underwear, socks and shoes on this project – which they are prepared to do because of the prestige of working with you and because they love the designs – but we must be conscious that there is a limit beyond which they will have to start pawning their briefcases.

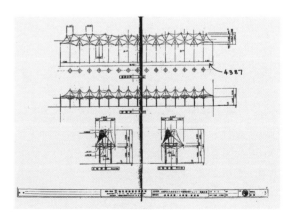

At the end of March Taiyo Tent were very anxious to start work.

To Simon Herron
From Tom Heneghan
26 March 1992

VERY URGENT

I am faxing because we urgently need your response to Kosugi. The lads are already on site and Taiyo need to order the steelwork immediately to meet the construction deadline. As I mentioned before, Taiyo are making no money (and almost certainly a loss) on Kosugi. The price for the fittings from their subcontractor came in at almost twice what they had anticipated – therefore they need to make some small changes …

Please confirm everything you can by return. Taiyo must order the steelwork immediately in order to meet the deadline. Don't bother to re-fax the drawings – just say (e.g.) sheet F2 – detail acceptable. I am sorry to have to rush you on this – basically it is because Taiyo have been working against a deadline and cost difficulties all the time and haven't been able to present you with this information until today. I assure you that they have been working all hours to get this far.

At the beginning of the second week in April the ground slab for the toilet block had been laid – on schedule – and Tom Heneghan faxed Simon Herron, asking him to choose one alternative for the umbrella safety-cable seam cover. Herron chose a standing seam.

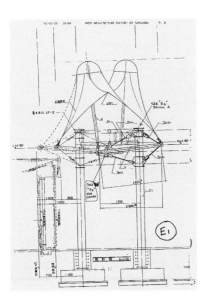
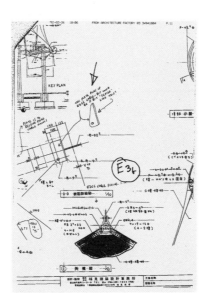
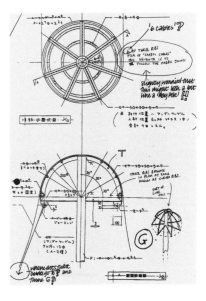

Problems: March–June 1992

The next months were quiet for the London end: in Japan the executive architects were working on the production drawings, the Taiyo Tent engineers on the structure and fabric. Working to a very tight budget, decisions were negotiated by fax over a number of details, for example the lighting. In mid May Heneghan faxed the Herrons with alternative details of the column-mounted uplighters and downlighters. He had gained agreement about the Herron's preference for substituting down lights with lights set in the pavement.

To Simon Herron
From Tom Heneghan
18 May 1992

Your local architect has proposed using lights which are 100 x 200 and 500 mm deep (the depth being set into the ground and the lights flush with the surface). These would not be powerful enough to floodlight the canopy (and would be blinding if they were) and he suggests either setting one inside each rear column, or one inside each front column – excluding one column at each end of the front row.

By 'inside each column' I mean as shown in the sketch below. The LA has calculated that we do not have enough money to afford more than eight lights.

However all this has to do with your decision – this is only a suggestion, please take it as nothing more than that – but we do need your decision urgently.

Back in London, the Herron office had looked at the plan for the ground-level lighting and the frustrations of not being there emerged. Ron Herron hand-wrote this fax to Tom Heneghan.

You know how I hate to nag but …

There are things that have been moved on the site plan that screw up (what was) a very elegant plan, i.e. the toilet block has moved towards the ramp and has taken the canopy with it … Now I know it's too late to do anything about this … but somehow some planting has popped up behind the toilets and some additional paving, etc.

I hate planting!! particularly the municipal kind … please/please get it removed!! …

Sorry to moan. I know it is not your fault.

Ron

PS. We have two drawings in the RA show this year – one Daimon, one Kosugi. [The Daimon drawing was to win the £1500 second prize in the AJ/Bovis Award for architecture at the 1992 Royal Academy Summer Exhibition.]

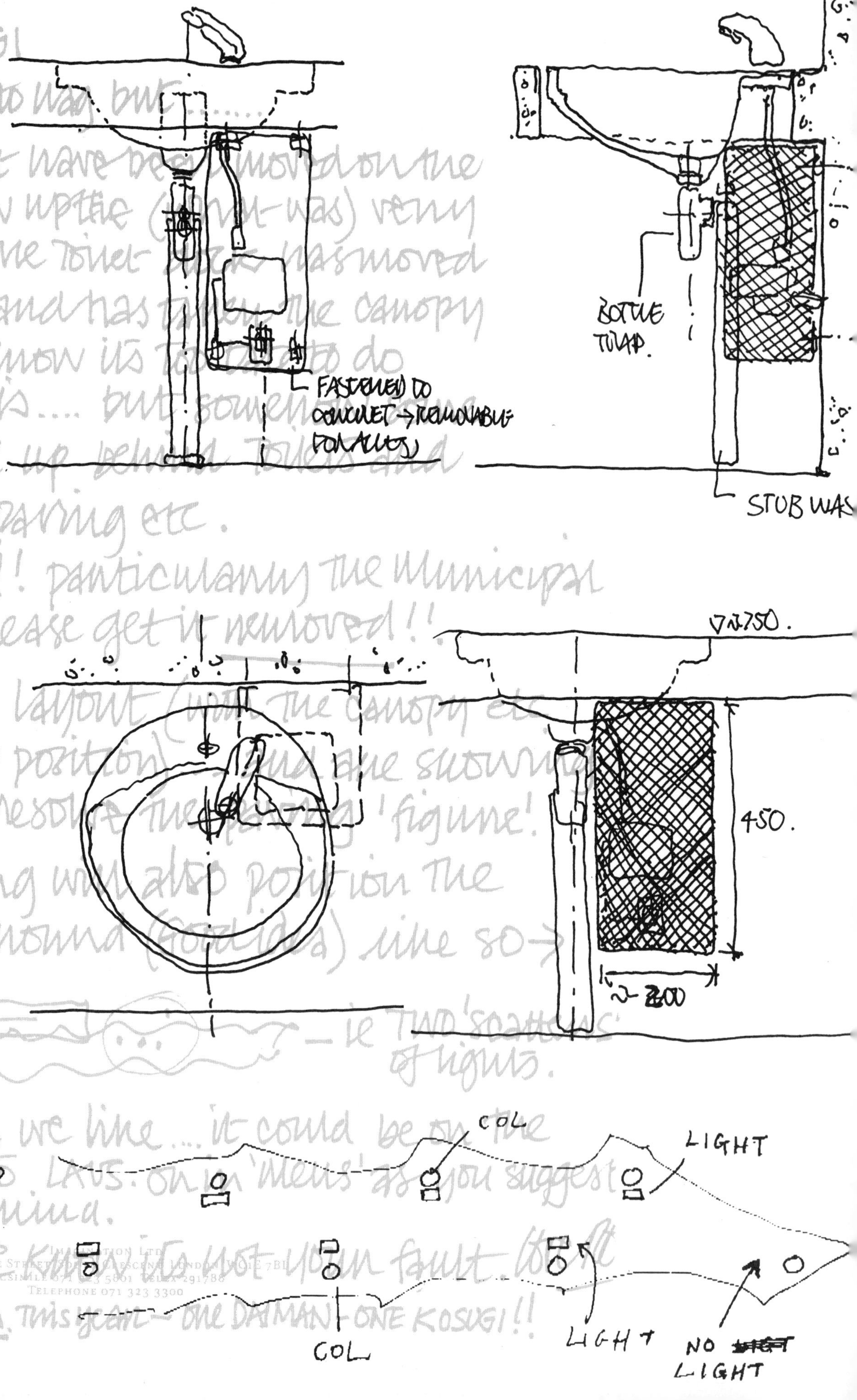

BOTTLE TULIP.

STUB WAS

FASTENED TO CONCRET → REMOVABLE FOR ALLES

∇ 1750.

450.

≈ 200

COL

LIGHT

COL

LIGHT   NO LIGHT

Heneghan replied in detail explaining that Kosugi wanted to get rid of the surrounding urban mess but had had to divert some of the 'demolition' budget in order to add money to the canopy-erection budget.

The Town also wants to remove most of this junk but they just don't have the money … but as soon as they can they will remove it … As for the other 'improvements', I explained that these had been approved and ordered by the Town before they commissioned the canopy and most cannot be cancelled – partly because it would need the full Council to agree …

The only consolation – as you will see when the photos arrive – is that the steel frame (even without the fabric) is so visually STRONG that it overpowers everything else and all the tattiness of the surroundings disappears … When the fabric arrives, the effect then is unimaginable (for me).

I'm not sure about the WC and canopy moving on the site plan – we sent you a copy in book form for final checking some weeks ago. Since I didn't hear from you I assumed that the basic layout was agreed.

With the contract due to end in late June, the faxes became longer, more detailed, finicky – and tenser. Heneghan was performing a brilliant role in acting as go-between for half-a-dozen foreign architects, some of them rather more _prima donna_ than the Herrons, on 16 projects. But as piggy in the middle, all the complaints and frustrations from abroad came to him.

In late March he fired a letter at all the foreign architects telling them to pull their socks up. Ron Herron, a long-time good friend of Heneghan, immediately telephoned, and Simon sent a private letter explaining how very much the team appreciated all Heneghan's help, his sleepless nights, and that any grumbles had not been directed at him or the Urban Factory. He wrote, quite truthfully, 'The Toyama projects are all total light, relief and pleasure – we are actually talking and discussing architectural issues.'

It was just as well the air had been cleared because at the beginning of June Kazuhiro Ando faxed saying that work on the basins and taps in the toilets had been stopped as Herron had instructed. He had been alerted to the fact that. shortly before. the Town had insisted that automatic taps were to be installed – together with their mechanisms. What was needed from the Herrons was agreement to this and to a plain grey painted panel under the sink to disguise the pump.

This caused a frisson in London because hiding the mechanisms was entirely against the spirit of the glass 'jewel'. Herron was firm about having a perforated metal enclosure and chrome waste fittings in place of the grey plastic which had been installed.

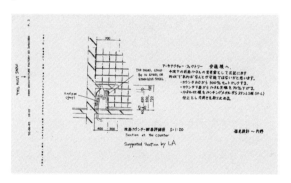

The other toilet problem was in explaining what granolithic flooring actually looked like and how it was made. After some translating and searching for suppliers it was eventually laid.

At the same time there had been uncertainties about the size of the paving tiles under the canopy – and in the relationship between their grid and the grid of the columns and that of the lavatories. In the end, largely because the tiles had been laid, the issue died.

The Kosugi 'drawing'exhibited at the 1991 Royal
Academy Summer Exhibition, a montage based on
Andrew Herron's computer model.

Almost there: June–September 1992

To Simon Herron
From Tom Heneghan
12 June 1992

Dear Simon
It's me writing today because Mr. Ando is floating around
the ceiling. He has just heard that he has won second prize
in an international ideas competition … Ando-san has to
wait for the official letter to arrive before telling anyone –
but you know me – I'm a blabbermouth and I have to tell
someone. Mr. Ando is a genius! Mr. Ando has just swooped
down for a second to remind me what I am really writing
about.

We have just received the latest snaps. The flying struts
are up, the WC glass blocks almost complete and I have to
say the whole thing looks A M A Z I N G ! Expo opens 10
July so all work is happening at speed and doubtless with a
few cock-ups – but the effect of the whole is so strong I
think you will probably be able to forgive most mistakes.

Then …

To Simon Herron
From Tom Heneghan
26 June 1992

URGENT

Well there had to be a major cock-up sometime. Kosugi was
going too well!

The fabric roof is up but the fabric between the ends of
each flying V strut has slightly greater curvature than your
drawing indicates and this – added to a structure-
positioning error, for which I must take full responsibility –
means that the edge of the tent does not fully shelter the
toilet door.

The Town is most concerned about the lack of cover over
the WC entrance where rain will be discharged from the
roof directly over the centre of the entrance.

Taiyo are very sorry about this problem. So are we. At
present we only have to solve the WC entrance problem.

**Taiyo Tent suggested some revisions which they were
prepared to construct at their own expense – even
though the problem had not principally been caused by
them. In the end the canopy looked so good, the expo
was only for the summer months and Taiyo Tent's
engineers had been so extraordinarily helpful that it was
decided to leave the problem until later.**

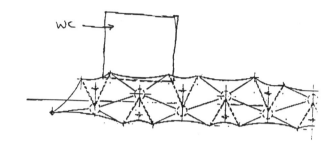

← THIS SKETCH SHOWS ROOF AS YOU DESIGNED.

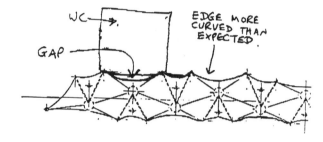

← THIS SKETCH SHOWS ROOF AS BUILT – WITH THE EDGES OF THE ROOF MORE CURVED THAN INTENDED – WHICH CREATES A GAP (APPROX 700 WIDE MAX) IN FRONT OF THE WC DOOR.

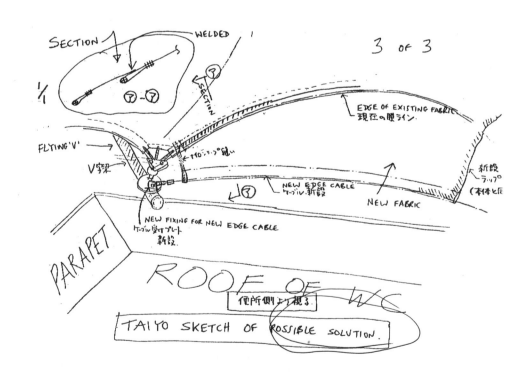

On Ron Herron's September 1992 trip, Tom Heneghan was unable to meet him at Tokyo for the train journey to Toyama and was very worried about his safe arrival.

I had to get there on my own. Tom had given me a bit of paper with four phrases to use at the railway stations. I waved them under people's noses and got there with very little hassle. We went straight to Kosugi and met with some of the council officers and then to the site and saw the canopy for the first time. The local architects were there and a TV crew and there were interviews. You have to make up answers out of the top of your head.

It was amusing and very exciting because you've had meetings and sent faxes and you've done the drawings – and suddenly it exists. It's very exciting, better than I had expected, very powerful, the canopy really floating over this over-sized steelwork which looked as if it could hold up a ten-storey building.

Then we went back to the town hall with the mayor who made a speech about how well the building had been received by the local people and how pleased he was and what might be the next step. I talked at great length about designing for change.

In the evening the mayor organized a bus. Half a mile away you could see the building beautifully lit by the scatter of lights in the pavement and the toilets like a lantern. I convinced them that they shouldn't alter the lighting – it was just perfect. And then back to Toyama.

Event Structure
Aug. 92'

need tents!
'voluptuous'

SHOP

IT'S A?

"ITS A-BEACH" - 1971

Monte Carlo Casino - 1971

temporary shopping sena

instant city May 69. LA.

gas station study - 1988

southampton 1988

Nadderlow
1990
NM

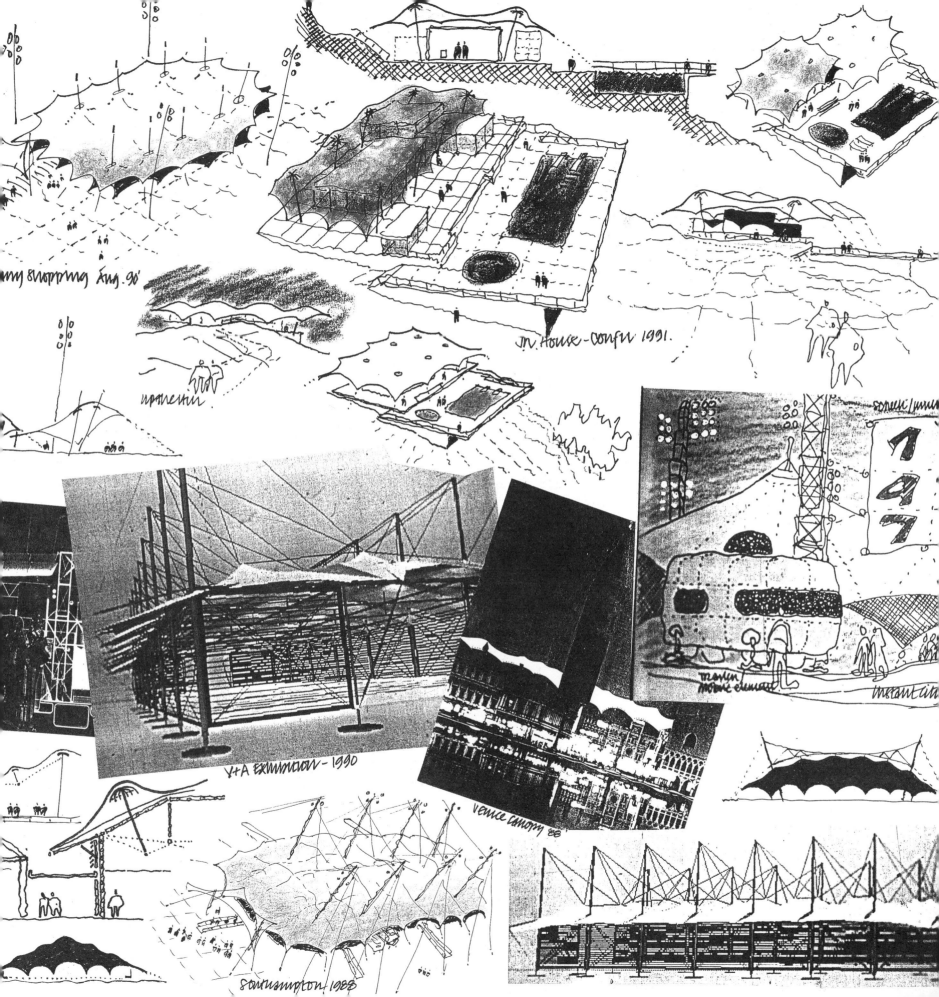

ny shopping Aug. 90'

In House-Corfu 1991.

V+A Exhibition - 1990

Venice Canopy 88

Southampton - 1988

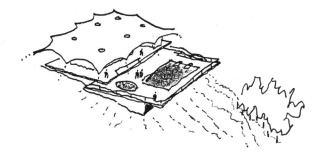

Kosugi

In conversation, Ron Herron talks about back-pocket ideas: that collection of design thoughts and schemes which never made it into reality because they were too extreme or the clients didn't like them or they ran out of cash – or which were ideas which had to be set down and worked out in the pages of the black cloth-bound A4 notebooks which Herron buys in bulk from the local stationers.

Forget the idea that his design is simply a rechurning of unrealized ideas. But, as he disarmingly puts it himself, 'There are a whole lot of things you have designed, details, big things, ways of doing things, ideas you never get to put into reality. And suddenly there's a possibility.'

Herron's interest in fabric structures goes back to the late 1960s. He and Archigram had been captivated by inflatables. There was a kind of magic in creating stable and strong structures by simply pumping air into a flexible skin. They could be anchored by filling similar bags with water. They could be put up and dismantled easily and moved around to practically any location in the back of a van. And they could be of practically any size you liked. In the 1960s at the Architectural Association and in other architecture schools all over the world thousands of inflatables were made with builders' polythene, gaffer tape and mum's vacuum cleaner with the hose in the other end.

For Herron at the time fabric canopy structures looked too unwieldy, they weren't easily transportable and they used a lot of rigid members. With Frei Otto's 1967 Montreal Expo canopy, his views began to change. Otto showed that fabric tension structures could be free-flowing in shape and they could, visually at least, float. And then it became clear that it was possible to use large free-form fabric structures as a non-specific semi-enclosure for a whole lot of other self-contained structures – as in, for example, Herron's 1968 canopy over St. Mark's, Venice, and his 1969 version of Instant City.

Canopies are a different animal, but they have a kind of consonance with Christo's wrapping of existing buildings and places in fabric for limited periods of time – an idea which Herron still finds absorbing. Both deploy soft materials and imply impermanence, transportability – and the possibility of providing on-the-spot, almost expedient, responses to specific, short-term issues.

Herron has been designing canopies ever since the 1960s. But in the late 1980s and early 1990s he has had a spate of design commissions on which he has worked with leading-edge engineers such as Ian Liddle of Buro Happold and Neil Thomas of Atelier One and, on the Toyama projects, the engineers of Taiyo Tent Company.

What in the 1960s looked seriously off the wall has, with new fabric technology and computerized engineering calculation, become a perfectly respectable branch of engineering design and manufacture. The client world doesn't necessarily see it that way yet – of a dozen commissions of these later years only the Imagination Building in London and the Toyama projects have so far been built.

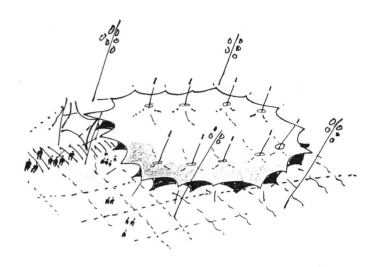

At Kosugi, Herron's earliest ideas were for a large fabric roof over the whole site with the mesh-wrapped package toilets and the underpass stair enclosure the loose elements underneath. Here was a straightforward first thought. The final design began to emerge as cost forecasts diminished the area of the canopy and the construction of the toilets, and as local structural safety factors beefed up the size of the members and the pitch of the canopy humps. Curiously, it has much more of the quality of a Pink Cloud than the earlier schemes, suspended (and at the same time supported) on a staggered row of raw industrial tubing by a mystifying cat's-cradle of struts and cables. At night they disappear, when from outside – and from several miles away over the flat plain – the canopy floats as an enigmatic glowing haze across the end of the station plaza.

Part of the intriguing quality of canopies such as this is that they represent the extreme support-plus-skin structural condition of frame buildings, here pared back to their most economical and, despite the taut softness of the fabric cloud, brutally expressed form.

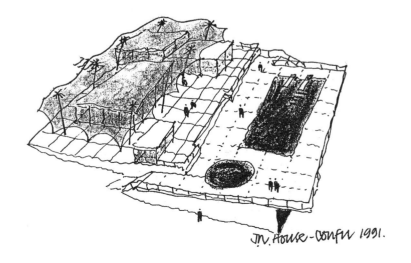

JN. House-Conn 1991.

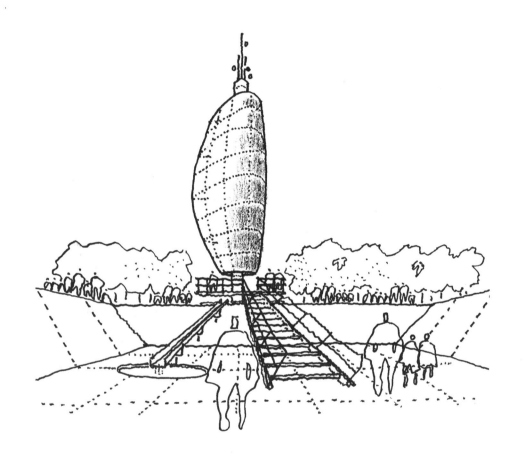

Kurobe

Kurobe is a town on a low-lying flood plain near the sea with snow-capped ski-resort mountains in the background. The area is criss-crossed by irrigation canals for the local rice fields. Snowfall is deep and typhoons a regular occurrence. Occasionally there are floods. At the edge of the town two converging rivers flow through rice fields, join up and then run a short distance into the sea.

The town wanted a tower reflecting the twin themes of wind and water at the apex of the triangular plot at the junction of the two canals – the end of a 22-hectare plot which had been earmarked as a large sports and recreation water park.

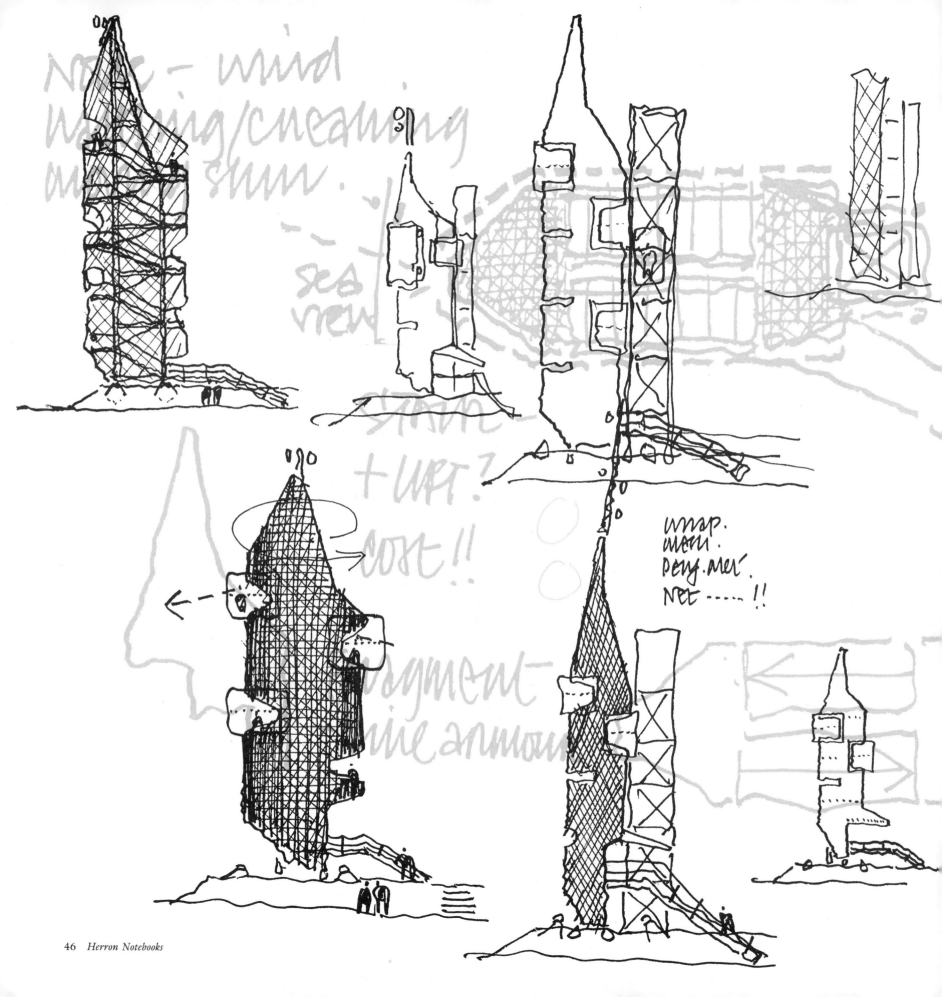

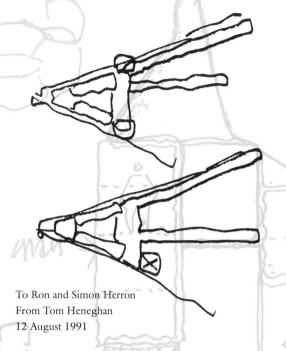

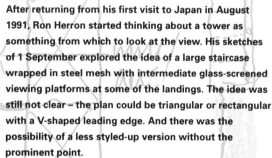

First ideas: 1 September 1991

The Herrons were free to select the precise location of the tower in conjunction with the town. There was no restriction about whether people could walk up to the top of the tower and it was not necessary for it to have a particular function except that it should exploit the windy conditions of the flat landscape and could possibly relate to the canals. Landscaping of the whole area was to be completed at a later time but the Herrons were asked to make suggestions for the landscape around the tower itself.

To Ron and Simon Herron
From Tom Heneghan
12 August 1991

This is not a romantic traditional Japanese town. In fact it is very modern and prosperous. The reason for its prosperity can be found at the front of your trousers – the zipper I mean. Check it. Doesn't it say YKK? Well maybe not, but you DO know YKK zippers. Over here they make considerably more than zippers – aluminium windows, panels, etc. Kurobe is YKK's base town. Now, YKK has a tradition of patronizing good architecture. All over Japan they have appointed top architects, but particularly in Kurobe where they built the YKK Guest House by Maki and they recently – get this – appointed an English architect to do a showpiece factory. The Kurobe budget is ¥440 million (approximately £150,000).

After returning from his first visit to Japan in August 1991, Ron Herron started thinking about a tower as something from which to look at the view. His sketches of 1 September explored the idea of a large staircase wrapped in steel mesh with intermediate glass-screened viewing platforms at some of the landings. The idea was still not clear – the plan could be triangular or rectangular with a V-shaped leading edge. And there was the possibility of a less styled-up version without the prominent point.

Towers are a different proposition from most architectural problems. They're objects in the sense that like the cube and the dome you can walk around them and see them all at once. They're something instantly readable, extruded spatially. And there's the problem of access and vertical circulation: as you go up you're popping into spaces rather than moving around.

But perhaps there should be a lift for disabled people which would introduce another element, and in that case perhaps the cladding could be varied with mesh around the leading edge and the rear landings, the stair area clad in perforated metal and the lift an open braced structure.

But maybe that was over-wrought. Seeking to simplify the idea produced a mesh-wrapped cylinder with an attached lift tower.

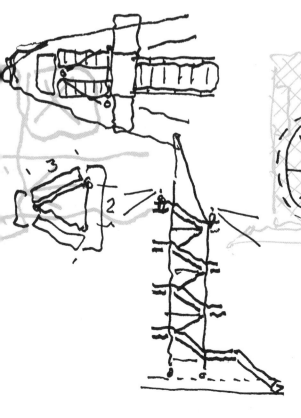

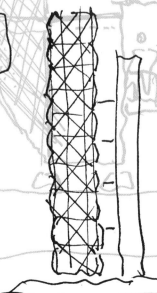

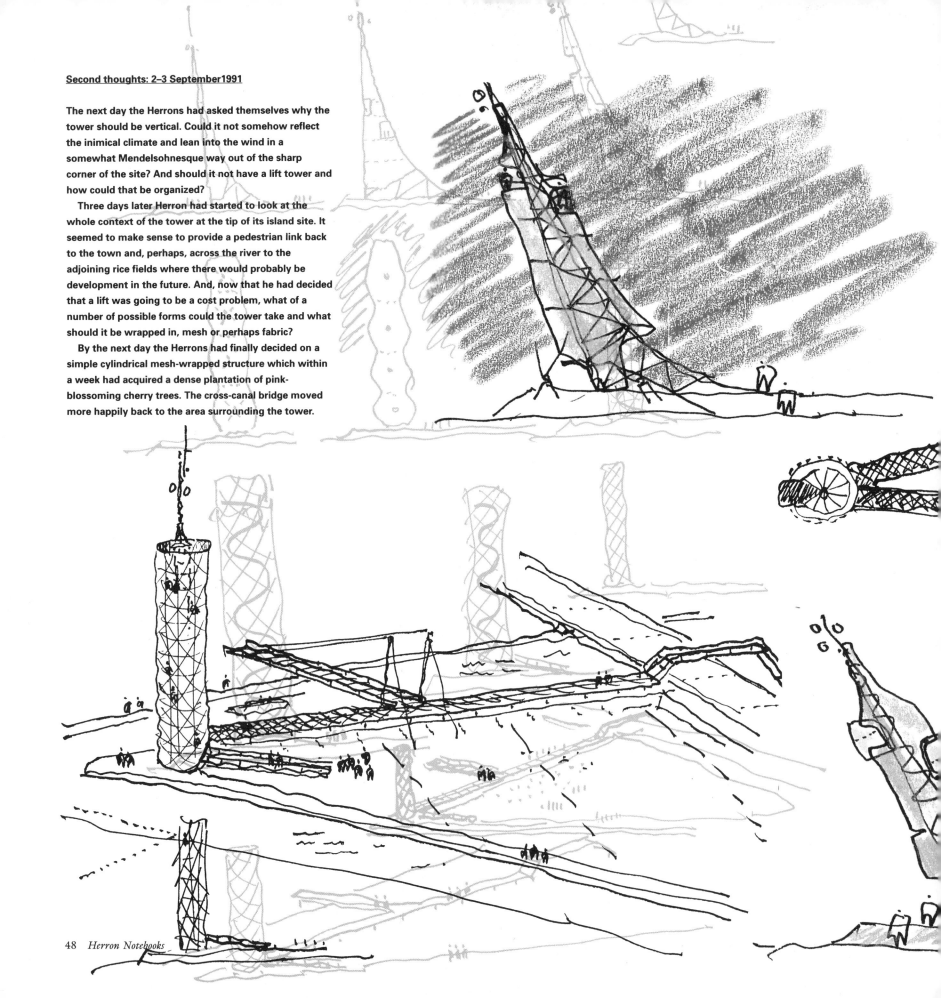

Second thoughts: 2–3 September 1991

The next day the Herrons had asked themselves why the tower should be vertical. Could it not somehow reflect the inimical climate and lean into the wind in a somewhat Mendelsohnesque way out of the sharp corner of the site? And should it not have a lift tower and how could that be organized?

Three days later Herron had started to look at the whole context of the tower at the tip of its island site. It seemed to make sense to provide a pedestrian link back to the town and, perhaps, across the river to the adjoining rice fields where there would probably be development in the future. And, now that he had decided that a lift was going to be a cost problem, what of a number of possible forms could the tower take and what should it be wrapped in, mesh or perhaps fabric?

By the next day the Herrons had finally decided on a simple cylindrical mesh-wrapped structure which within a week had acquired a dense plantation of pink-blossoming cherry trees. The cross-canal bridge moved more happily back to the area surrounding the tower.

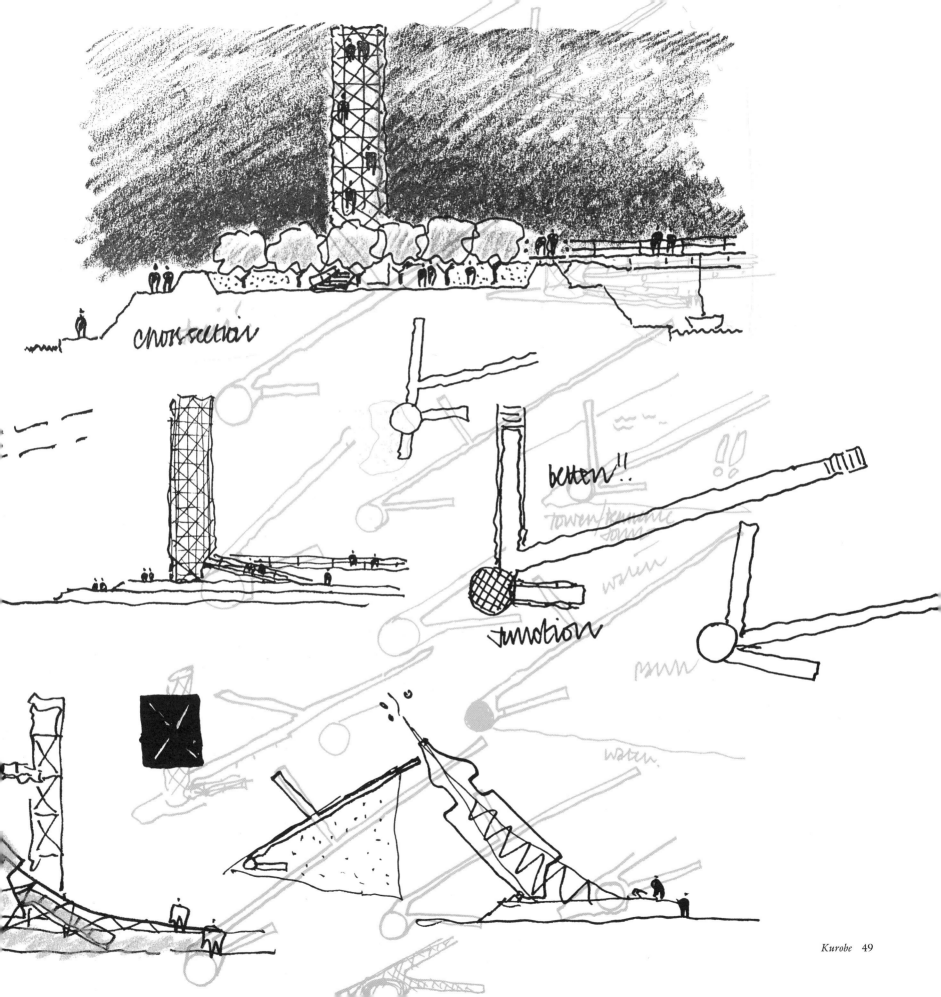

crossection

better!!..

junction

First presentation: October 1991

The outline sketches the Herron office sent to Tom
Heneghan at the beginning of October were for a simple
mesh cylinder around an internal stairway linked back to
the town via an aerial walkway through a new wood of
tightly planted cherry trees. At the tower a ramp led back
to ground level and a bridge to one side spanned the
adjoining canal.

   In Japan Tom Heneghan wasn't entirely sure that this
would be the final design.

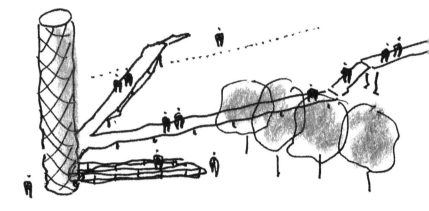

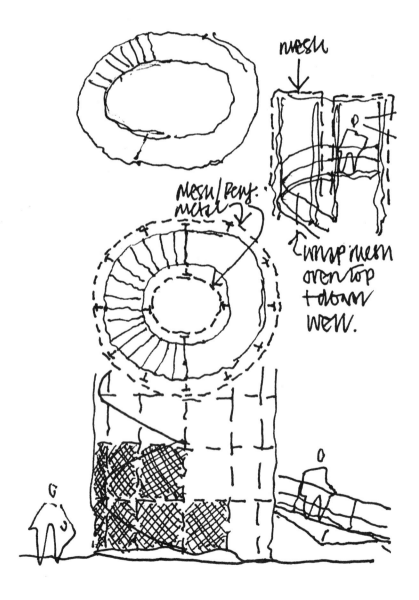

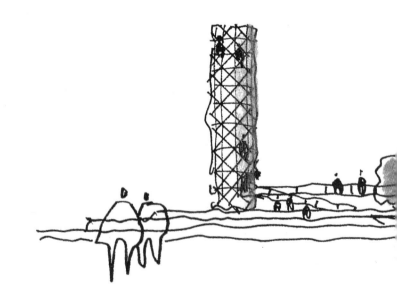

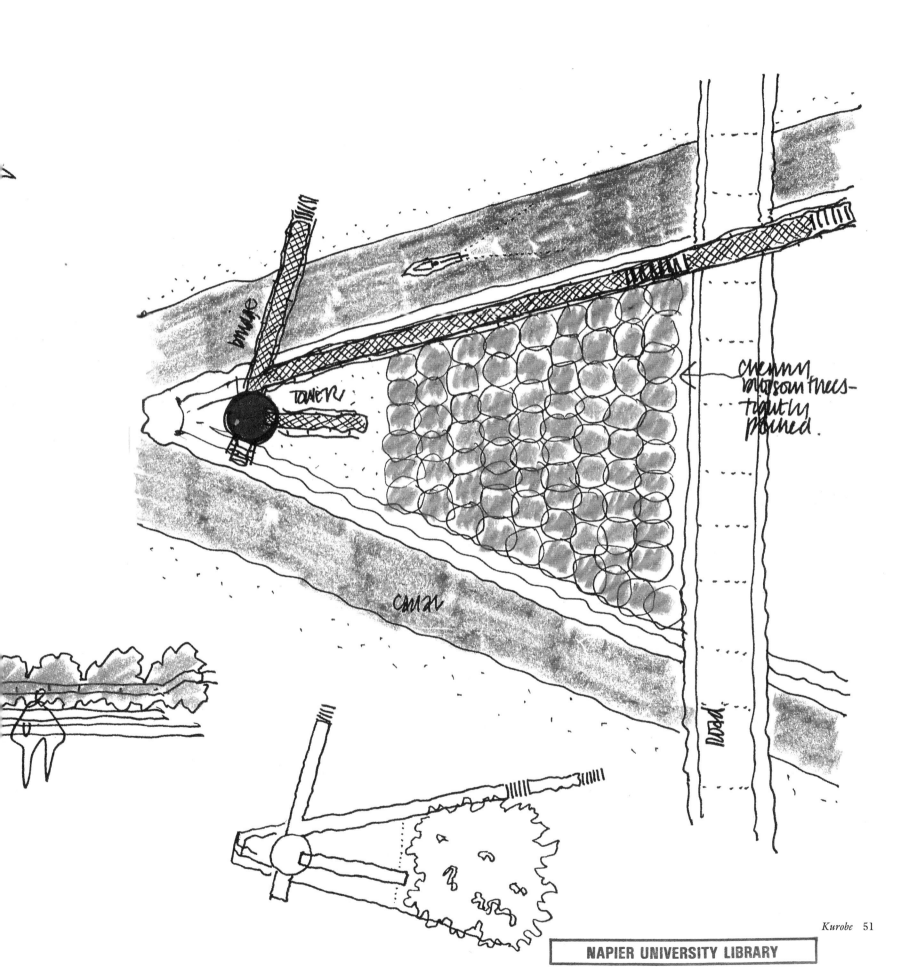

mure

TOWER

cherry blossom trees - tightly pruned.

canal

road

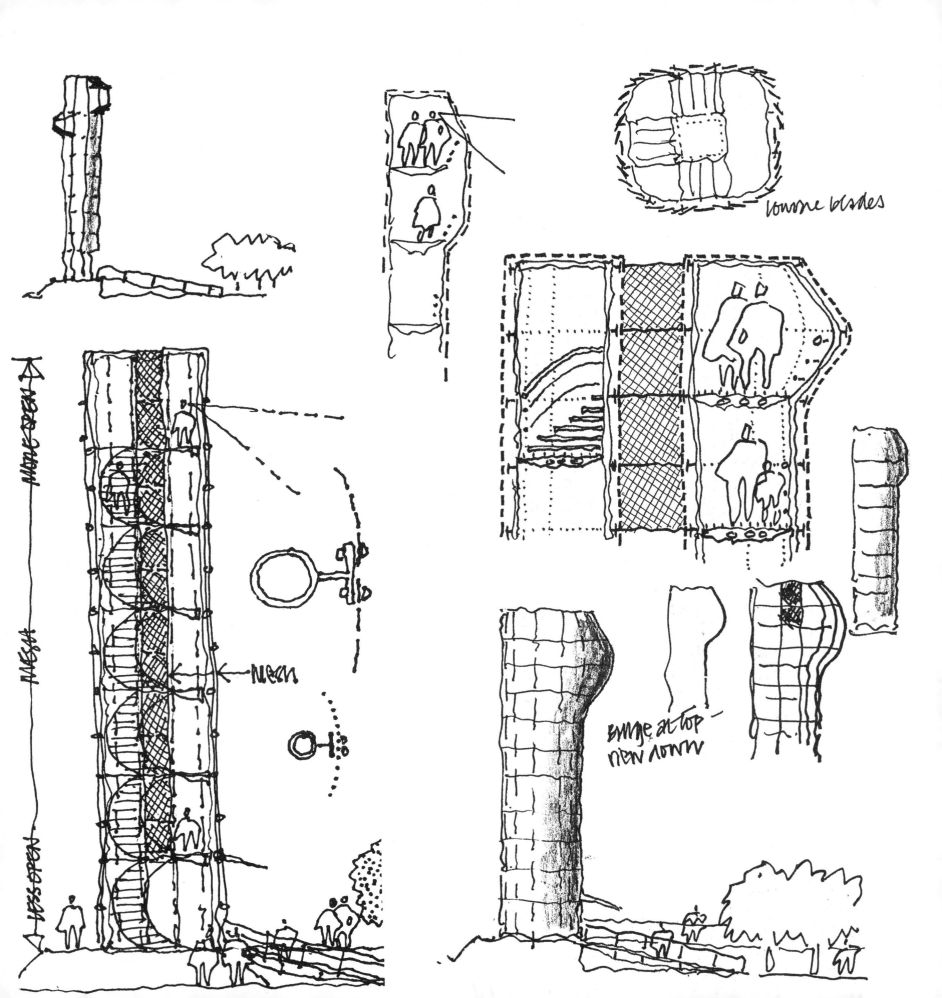

louvre blades

mesh

image at top
new town

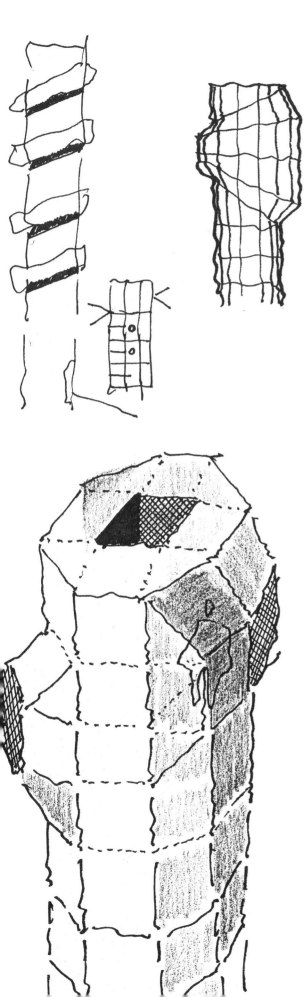

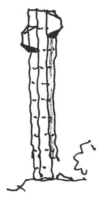

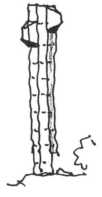

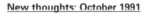

New thoughts: October 1991

Straight after sending the first ideas, Herron started worrying about the detail, varying the frequency of the mesh to make it almost opaque at the bottom, more open at the top. And one of the deliberate effects would be the inevitable rattling of the mesh in the wind. But perhaps a simple cylinder was too simple. Perhaps there should be a bulge at the top where people could sit or stand to take in the view. Alternatively, the tower could be octagonal with several viewing positions near the top. And another possibility might be to allow views out to the surrounding countryside only at the top by using ring or perhaps vertical louvres.

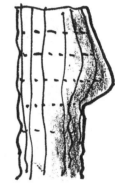

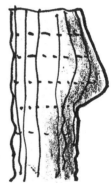

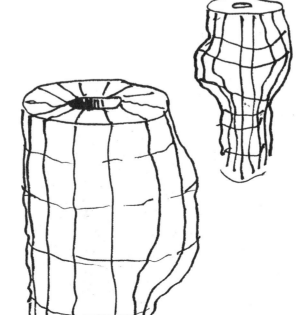

Change of tack: October 1991

By the end of the month things had moved on: there were more detailed things to sort out as the Urban Factory's advisor Toshiki Kato explained. The proposed bridge across the canal led to somebody else's land – on which Kurobe could not build. In addition, the proposed route of the walkway was along the canal bank. That would mean long discussions with the national rivers authority or the ministry of construction.

But there was a potential up-side: the Kurobe masterplan had not yet been approved by the council so that the Herrons could make a proposal without reference to the existing masterplan.

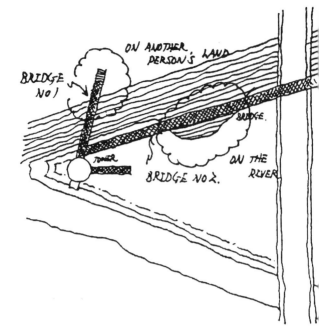

To James Philipps
From Tom Heneghan
31 October 1991

Hello James, etc.
Kurobe has accepted that your total triangular site should be landscaped according to your ideas. But if you insist on it being planted in this financial year then your tower budget must also cover the trees. So, obviously, you don't insist this year. Building on the riverbank is difficult because it is controlled by another body and it is not possible for them to negotiate with the town – I don't know why, I just work here. Anyway, since you are (I assume) working at a possible-strategies level I don't suppose any of this will cause you problems.

At the same time the Herrons had not been terribly satisfied with the static form of the tower, especially because it failed to address the possibilities created by the local high winds. It seemed sensible to allow the whole tower to respond to air movements. So by the second half of October they had started thinking about a rotating fabric-wrapped airfoil. James Philipps ended a fax to Heneghan with the enigmatic information, 'On Kurobe tower – we're working on making it move'.

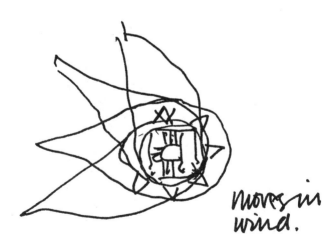

moves in wind.

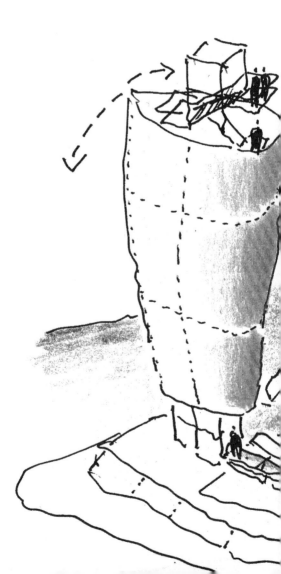

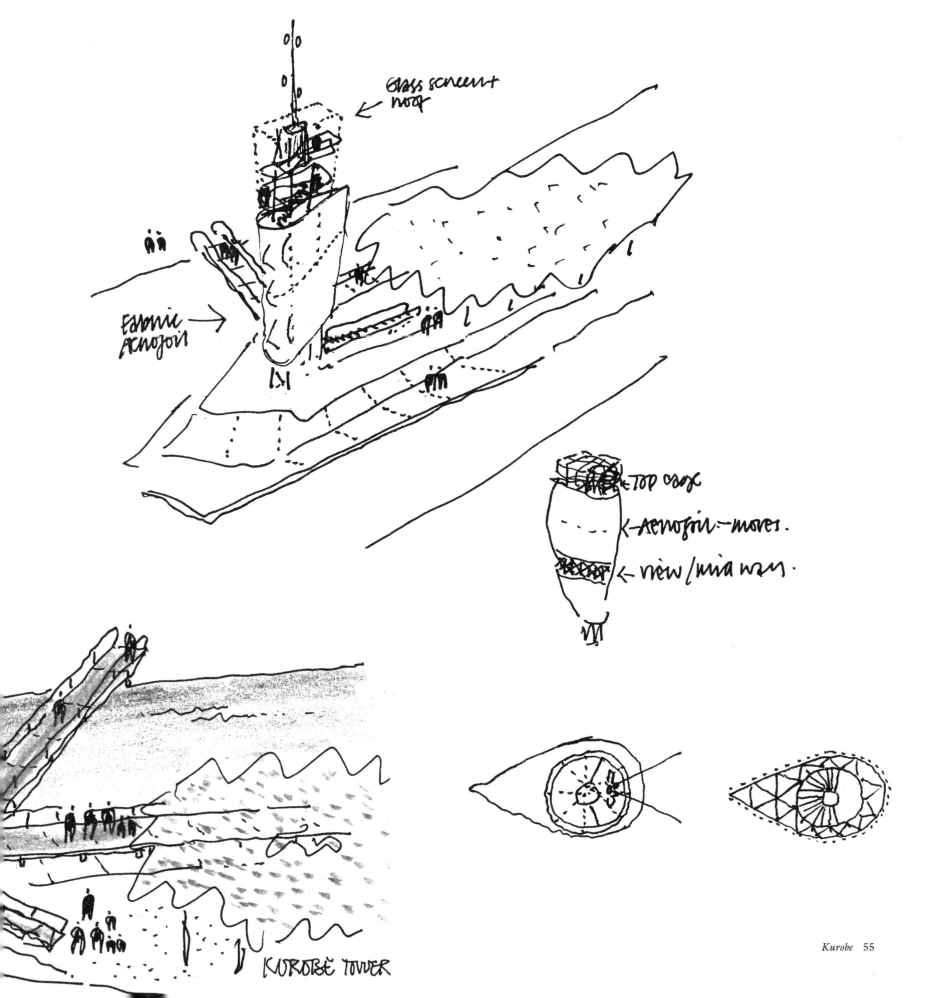

glass screen +
← roof

Esonic
Acrofoil →

← TOP csox

← Acrofoil — moves.

← view / min way.

KUROBE TOWER

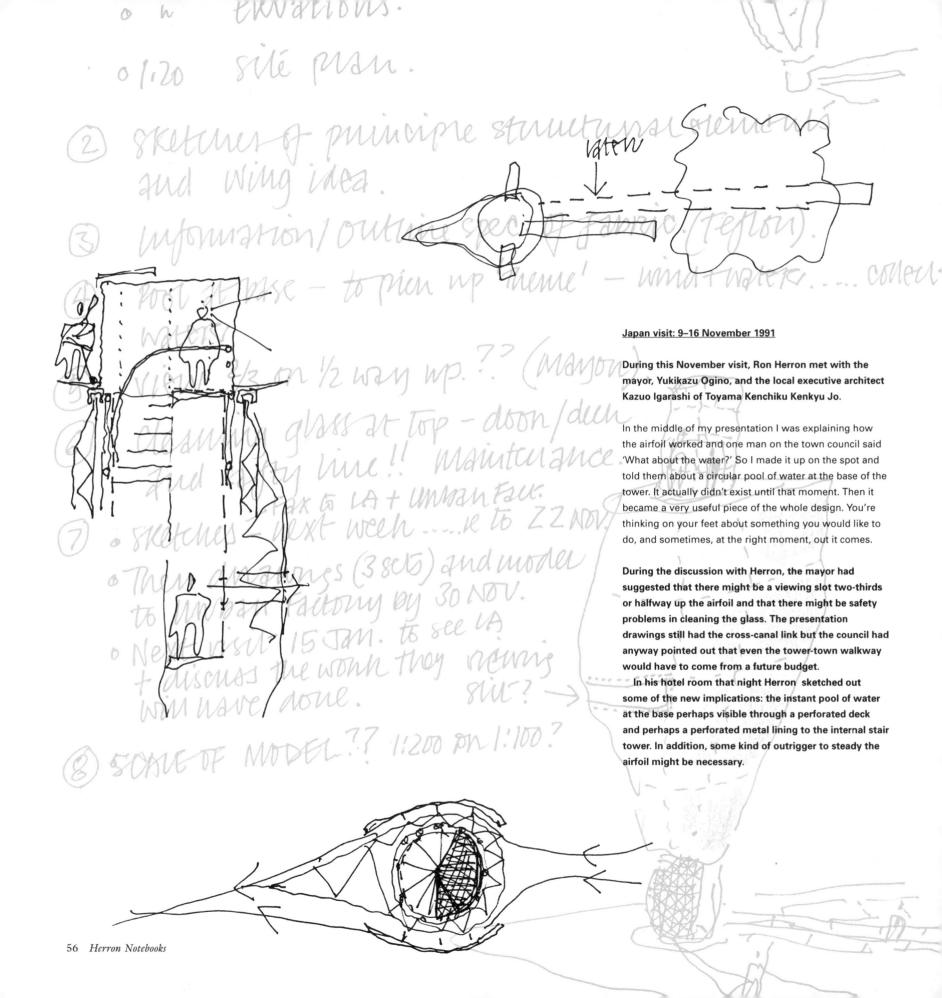

Japan visit: 9–16 November 1991

During this November visit, Ron Herron met with the mayor, Yukikazu Ogino, and the local executive architect Kazuo Igarashi of Toyama Kenchiku Kenkyu Jo.

In the middle of my presentation I was explaining how the airfoil worked and one man on the town council said 'What about the water?' So I made it up on the spot and told them about a circular pool of water at the base of the tower. It actually didn't exist until that moment. Then it became a very useful piece of the whole design. You're thinking on your feet about something you would like to do, and sometimes, at the right moment, out it comes.

During the discussion with Herron, the mayor had suggested that there might be a viewing slot two-thirds or halfway up the airfoil and that there might be safety problems in cleaning the glass. The presentation drawings still had the cross-canal link but the council had anyway pointed out that even the tower-town walkway would have to come from a future budget.
   In his hotel room that night Herron sketched out some of the new implications: the instant pool of water at the base perhaps visible through a perforated deck and perhaps a perforated metal lining to the internal stair tower. In addition, some kind of outrigger to steady the airfoil might be necessary.

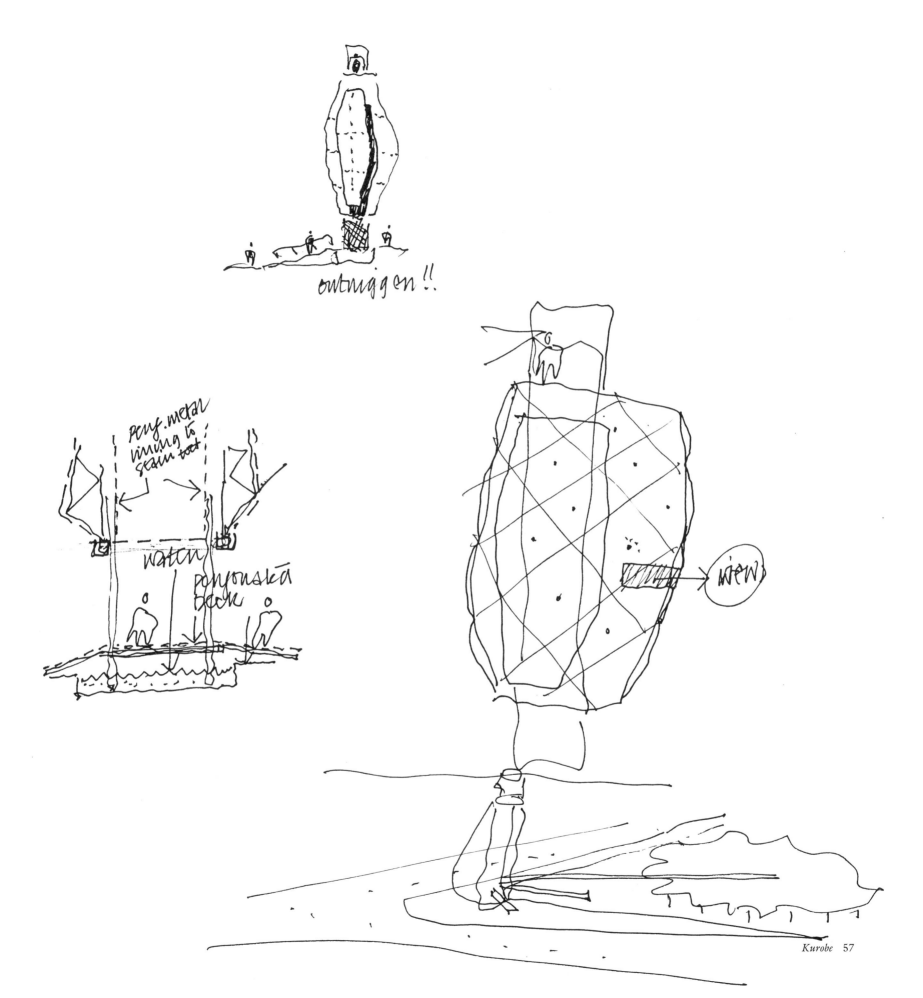

outrigger!!

perf. metal lining to stair foot

watch

ponyonska
beck

view

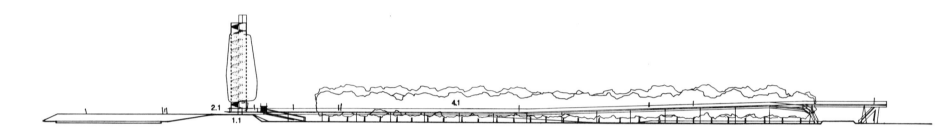

1:1000

1:500

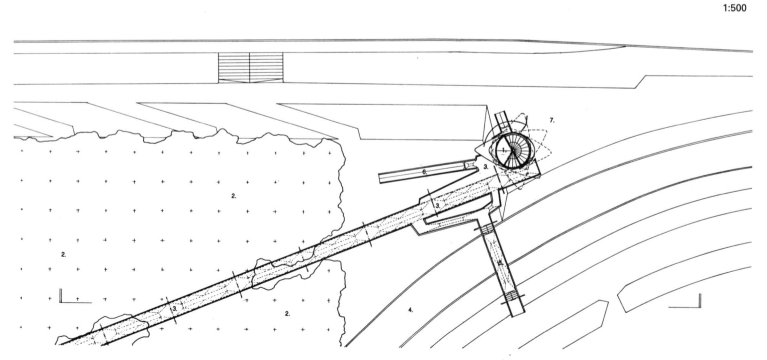

Presentation: 9–16 November 1991

The design they presented and had accepted was for a tower with a 25-metre-high structural steel core of ring beams and posts stiffened by the 4.5-metre diameter internal spiral stair with ten intermediate landings. The Teflon fabric airfoil on its own structure, yet to be worked out, rotated around this, leaving a section of stairway and a viewing platform rising from the top.

On his 9–16 November visit to Toyama Ron Herron took a set of drawings to Kurobe with a big sheet of selected preliminary sketches, a model and a poetic description of the project.

The tower reflects the mood of the winds – it rotates and flexes as the prevailing wind changes in direction and strength. The fabric wing structure is semi-translucent Teflon wrapped around a lightweight aluminium frame set on bearings fixed to a central steel stair core. Perforated metal panels act as wind breakers around the base of the tower, obscuring and limiting views. A glass enclosure atop the core provides shelter from driving wind and rain but allows a sense of exposure. Acting as a beacon lit from within the skin, the sail will appear to be floating and when viewed from a distance the play of frames will become apparent, the sail and frame moving over the central core.

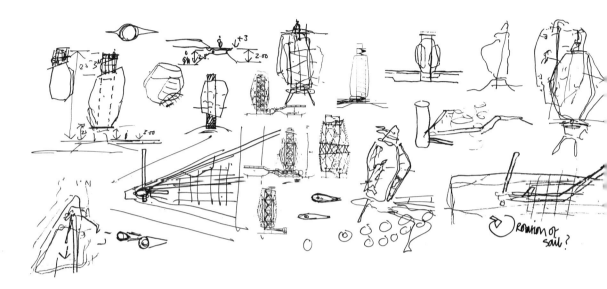

1:2000

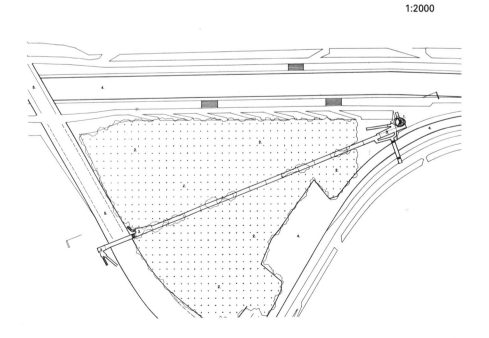

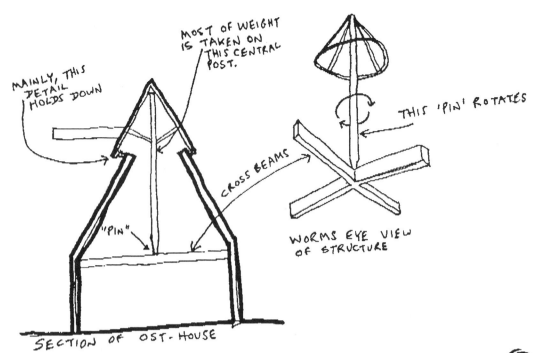

MAINLY, THIS DETAIL HOLDS DOWN

MOST OF WEIGHT IS TAKEN ON THIS CENTRAL POST.

THIS 'PIN' ROTATES

CROSS BEAMS

"PIN"

WORMS EYE VIEW OF STRUCTURE

SECTION OF OST-HOUSE

LOUSY DRAWING No ①

YES GUYS! - I DO KNOW THAT THIS ANGLE STINKS!

SPACE-FRAME AEROFOIL DISH

I HAVE NO IDEA HOW THE BOTTOM WORKS!
EXCEPT - I SUPPOSE THE WHOLE THING IS ON A TURNTABLE.
EXCEPT - THAT MAKES OVERTURNING A PROBLEM - SO I SUPPOSE STAIRCASE CORE IS FIXED, AND BECOMES THE 'POST' OF THE MERRY-GO-ROUND.

LOUSY DRAWING N②

ACTUALLY - I SUPPOSE A CONSTRUCT DEALS WITH THIS PROBLEM ALL T
SO - NO PROBLEM!!

Reaction from Japan: November 1991

To Herron Associates
From Tom Heneghan
18 November 1991

Dear All

I attach a formal response from the Urban Factory but you should understand that this masks great admiration and enthusiasm for your proposals. Anyway the problem with your Kurobe scheme is that it is not possible to think about anything else. I have spent hours and hours thinking about it when I should have been thinking about my own scheme. So this letter is to try to exorcise Kurobe from my brain. Well. I was thinking about the rotating sail and thinking about those rotating cowls on the top of old farmyard oast houses. They are structured like my fabulous sketch (1).

If your staircase does not rotate (and I imagine that is a bit difficult) then there must be a separate structure for the sail. Probably the sail can rotate on a number of circular tracks which are attached at a number of levels around the staircase. But maybe kids' fingers could get in there. I thought one answer might be Ron's suggestion that there would be slot windows in the fabric so that you didn't have to climb to the top to get a view. So maybe the fabric would go higher than the staircase and you could then support the fabric framework in a sort of merry-go-round detail from the top of the staircase – see my fabulous sketch (2).

That's all I wanted to say – now I can get back to my squid garden.

So, much love from the Architecture Factory (a Division of Crude Detailing, Inc.).

On 23 November the Herrons sent revised drawings to
Tom Heneghan showing a simplified viewing platform
with a safety walkway around the glass enclosure and
the pool indicated.

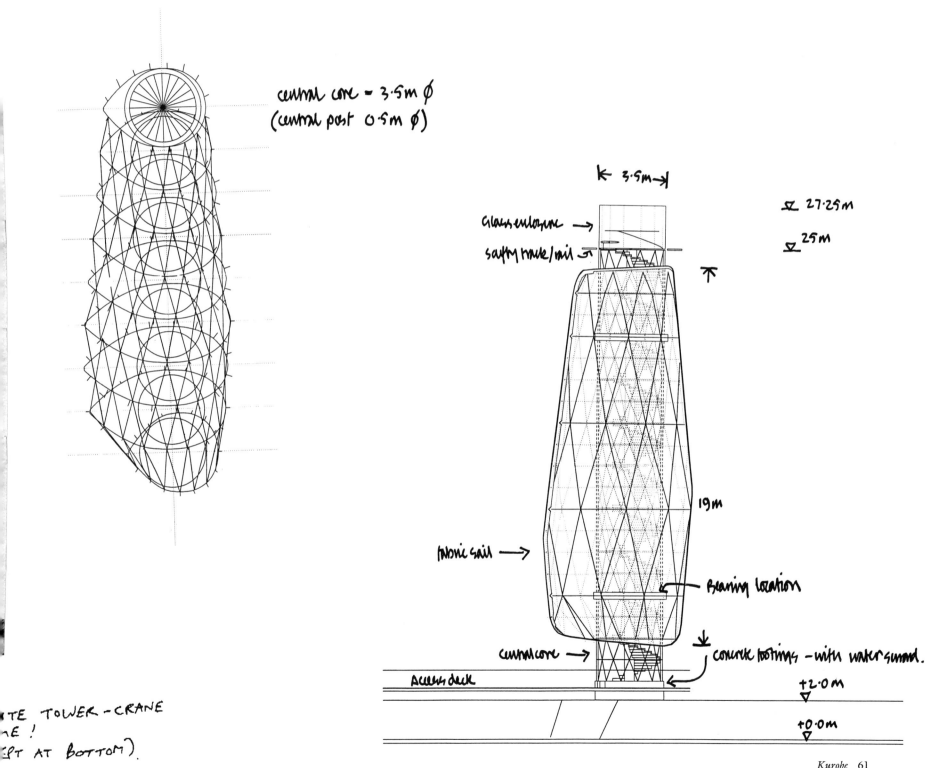

central core = 3.5m ⌀
(central post 0.5m ⌀)

⊢ 3.5m ⊣

▽ 27.25m

▽ 25m

Glass enclosure →

safety track/rail →

19m

fabric sail →

Bearing location

central core →

concrete footings – with water guard.

Access deck

+2.0m

+0.0m

TE TOWER – CRANE
...E !
PT AT BOTTOM).

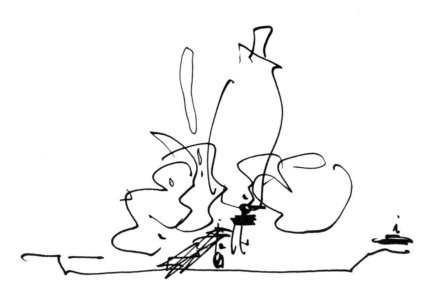

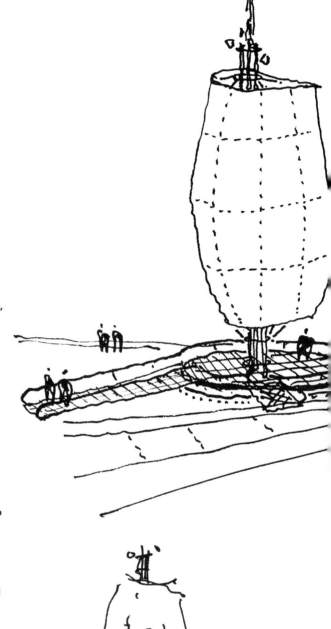

Breakthrough: November 1991

Three days later came depressing news. Construction costs in Japan were of a different order from British prices. The 25-metre-high staircase tower alone would cost around ¥450 million. The total project budget was ¥437 million.

Heneghan concluded his fax gently.

These figures obviously cause great problems for you and we appreciate that it will probably be difficult for you to send the drawings on 30 November. We are very sorry to have to bring you this news.

That day Anthony Leung from the Herron office faxed Heneghan with the news that Ron had been sketching new proposals.

He has had a re-think on access to the tower after comments made by the mayor. I attach a copy from his sketchbook which shows a leaner non-access tower. It will be of a similar airfoil shape and be able to rotate in the wind but will be closed to the public.

The idea is that the tower will be sitting on pool of water with a curtain of water around the base – suggesting that the tower is floating on a column of water. With lighting inside, it should be quite interesting.

We shall be pushing forward with this new idea, together with your comments about the costs. As you can understand, we shall not be able to send the tower drawings on 30 November and it would be much appreciated if you could let us have a revised date.

Refinements: November–December 1991

So far, the Herron thinking had been about a viewing tower but the potential cost problems made them reassess that. The brief had been non-committal so in Japan Ron had asked the Kurobe mayor, Yukikazu Ogino, whether he wanted a prospect tower. Although he had suggested a viewing slot about halfway up the presentation scheme, he was quite relaxed about the simple idea of a tower. While this gave the tower almost no ostensible working function, the confirmation enabled them to start developing the idea of a central support-only mast for the airfoil.

On 28 November Ron Herron and James Philipps had gone to Bristol University for a discussion with an aerodynamics expert about the feasibility of the airfoil section. Professor Lawton's view was that it was about right and he gave them a set of calculations based on a similar structure on which he had worked earlier. He also suggested that they introduce a damper to stop flutter. The obvious thing was to add a horizontal paddle in the circular pool of water around the base of the tower.

We made this airfoil without any real idea of how it could work. Professor Lawson pointed out that a pool might be the answer to flutter. As it happened we had the pool at the base I'd invented during the November presentation. The interesting thing was that they wanted a tower which responded to wind and water. Early on in a design you're struggling. I had got interested in the idea of a fabric canopy for Kosugi and out of that emerged the idea of a fabric-covered tower. One way or another projects go through these stages. Sometimes things don't make much sense and then another argument brings us back to it.

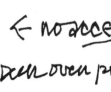

← no acce
dem oven po
pool + pa

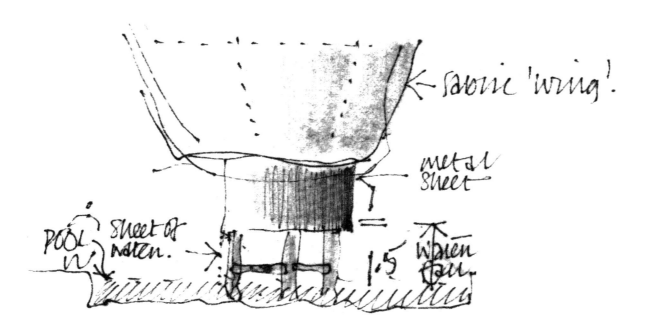

fabric 'wing'.

metal sheet

POOL sheet of water.

1.5 water

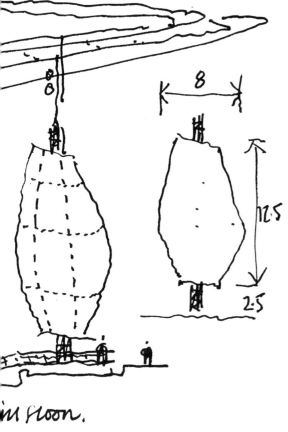

8

12.5

2.5

in floor.

Heneghan immediately got rough prices based on Herron's outline sketch.

To Ron Herron
From Tom Heneghan
29 November 1991

There appears to be one company holding a monopoly on supply of Teflon fabric in Japan – which affects the price. I expect that, while we might be able to buy the fabric cheaper in the USA or the UK, it would be difficult to erect it without the cooperation of the specialist Japanese company, so we will probably have to accept Japanese prices.

This estimate suggests that the budget will be tight even for the new design. We would like to suggest two possibilities:

(a) Maybe the height of the tower could be reduced, while keeping the proportions as you designed (or, we also like the fatter version of your October sketches – it reminds us of blowfish which you often see as dried inflated skins in Japanese restaurants). Since the tower no longer has a spiral staircase it could be possible to reduce the diameter and reduce the height proportionally. We would suggest that, even if the height is reduced to 12–15 metres, the effect will still be considerable since cherry trees usually only grow four to five metres high and this is a very flat site.

(b) Perhaps you could prepare a version which has parts of the sail formed from perforated (or unperforated) aluminium sheet, reducing the quantity of Teflon, and we could then try to obtain the aluminium as a donation from YKK. However, it would also be good for you to keep in mind a version which does not necessarily rely on an aluminium donation.

To Tom Heneghan
From James Philipps
29 November 1991

We are looking at simplifying the Kurobe sail and platform still further in light of a conversation Ron and I had with the aerodynamics professor T. Lawson at Bristol University. We are also contacting Sheetfabs (the people who did the bridges, fabric structure, etc., here at Imagination) just to see what sort of cost we would be looking at to supply and fix in Japan – it may be noticeably cheaper.

With reference to your Kurobe point (a), we would prefer to maintain the maximum height – but obviously if it is the only way …

Kurobe point (b): yes it's possible to replace sections with another material – however the additional loading, additional structure, etc., will probably result in hardly any saving.

To James Philipps
From Tom Heneghan
2 December 1991

Kurobe – yes, I'm afraid we think at this stage it is probably best to try to reduce the tower to a maximum of 15 metres or less. Then if there is money remaining we can be more elaborate at the lower levels and have more elaborate add-ons at a higher level.

Final presentation: December 1991

On 17 December the Herrons sent revised formal drawings to Tom Heneghan with a model and computer model. This was more or less the final scheme from which the detail drawings were worked up by the local architects and the fabric firm. The airfoil had been reduced in height from 19 metres to around 14 metres although the top of the mast reached above 21 metres. The long semi-aerial walkway through the cherry blossoms would have to wait for later funding.

The pool, now a metre deep, to accommodate the anti-flutter paddle, had a long run-off channel ramping down to the beginning of the cherry-tree wood.

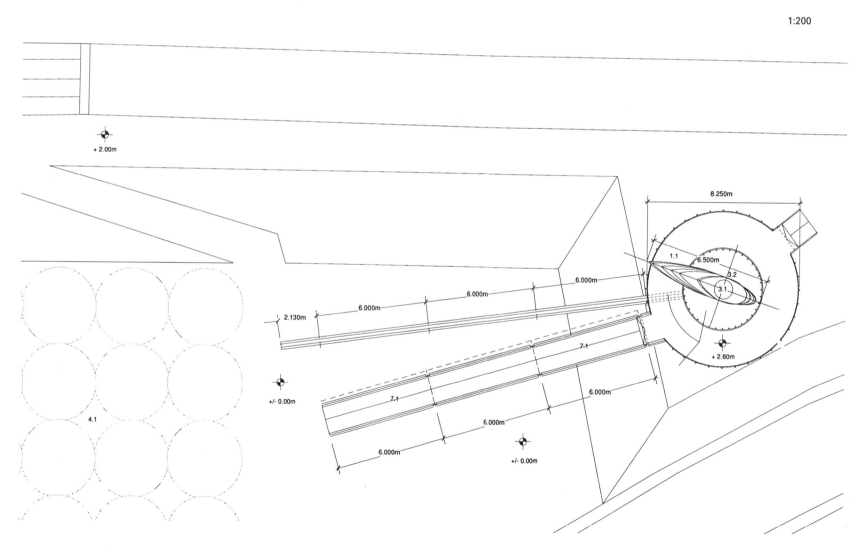

1:200

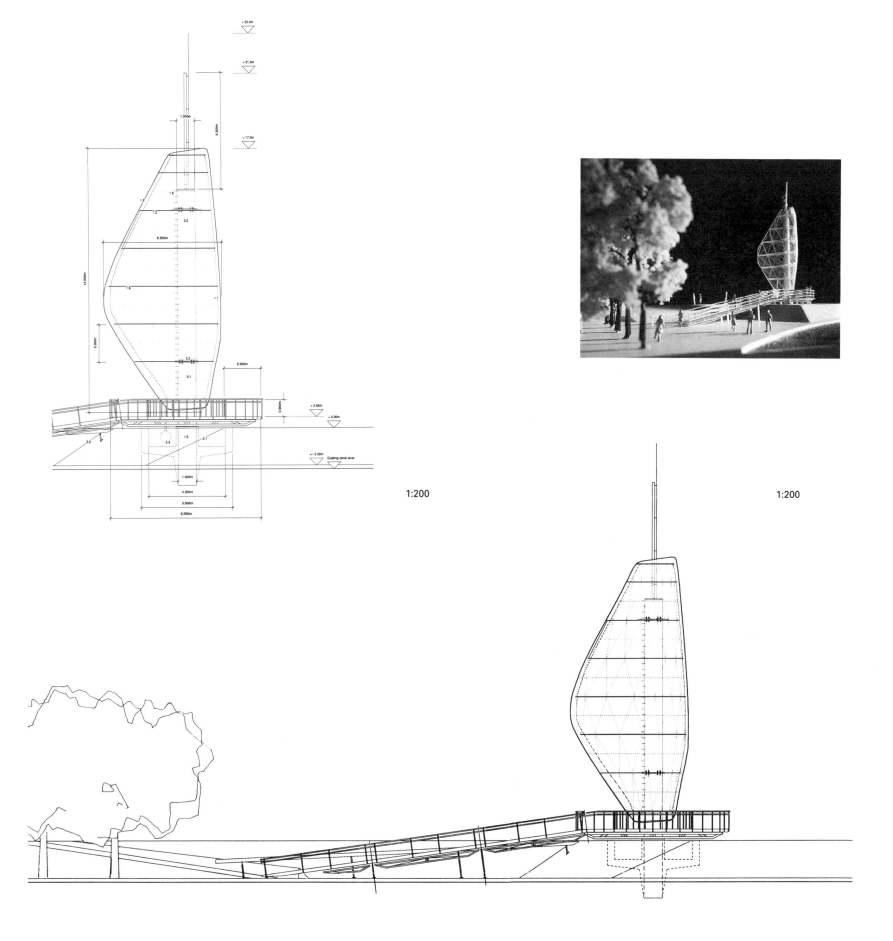

+ 23.0m

+ 21.0m

+ 17.0m

6.200m

1.000m

1.5

1.3

3.2

6.500m

14.000m

1.6

1.1

2.000m

3.2

5.1

2.000m

0.900m

+ 2.60m

+ 2.00m

2.2

3.3

1.2

2.1

+/- 0.00m

Existing canal level

1.000m

4.200m

5.000m

8.250m

1:200

1:200

Japan visit: February 1992

Delayed on a trip by an airport strike in Cyprus, Herron had the office send detail sketches of the decking surrounding the base of the tower, specified white as the colour for all the steelwork and promised a new site plan showing the agreed position for the tower only a few metres away from its original position.

By the middle of January the Urban Factory had obtained rough prices and discussed the project with Taiyo Tent: Kurobe at last looked to be on target.

Ron Herron made his third visit between 29 January and 9 February 1992.

I went through the formalities of updating the councils and the mayors. They are being faced with what in their terms are very odd buildings but to a man they have supported the projects.

The Kurobe mayor says he has the tower model on his office desk and is beginning to understand what I'm about and feels that the tower, although it has no function, will spark off architectural thinking in the town in the future.

We got into a talk about planning and he asked why planning always seemed to be about fixing things permanently. I said Japan was about the temporary and change and renewal and talked about the notion of the responsive plan.

At the next day's meeting, the town's engineers wanted to move the tower. Somebody hadn't picked up on the need for flood control: the site was at times below water level and levee banks protecting the site from the canals on either side were necessary. Herron was then able to say this was going to screw everything up. At this point Shuichi Fujie smoothly offered a trade-off: Herron would agree to the move but they would, in return, allow him to go ahead with the carpet of cherry trees.

The next meeting was with the admirable Taiyo Tent engineers with their preliminary engineering drawings. One of them pulled out a copy of the 1970 Archigram book and asked Herron to autograph it. The good news they brought was that they had found a perforated white fabric: 'Wonderful, better than we had hoped for' said Herron when he returned.

The Herron scheme for Kurobe was published in one of the local Toyama newspapers. Within a few weeks, as Tom Heneghan noticed as he was driving though Toyama City, an enterprising local retailer had mounted not one but two wire-frame models of the tower above his shop.

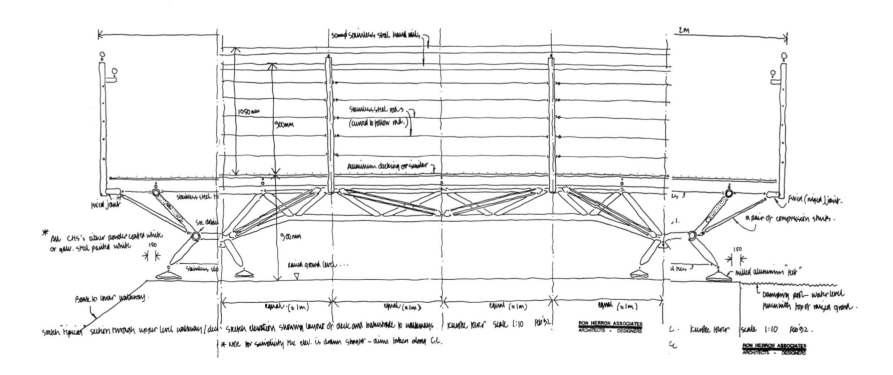

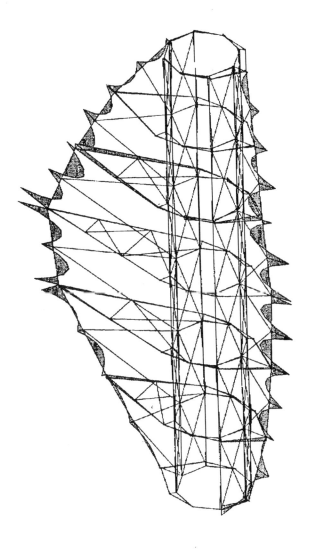

Engineering: March 1992

Near the end of March Taiyo had developed the engineering drawings.

To Simon Herron
From Tom Heneghan
26 March 1992

Taiyo are calculating to make the sail rotate at a wind speed of between 2 and 3 metres per second, aiming for closer to 2m/s. This is in a reasonable, but not strong wind. 1 m/s cannot be achieved.

In order to rotate at this speed the frame must be as delicate as possible – but as I mentioned in an earlier fax, any flutter paddle sticking in the water will create twisting stresses between the bottom and the top of the frame and the frame will consequently have to be made heavier and the sail move less. Taiyo would prefer no paddle or only a finger which ripples the water. As far as anyone knows, no-one has done anything like this before so it may be that there will be a flutter. Taiyo hope to control this in the bearings – but it is almost impossible really to know what will happen until it is on site. Taiyo understand but are not over-concerned about flutter. Anyway, flutter or not, Taiyo suggest that there is no paddle for the reasons above. Your confirmation is now very urgent.

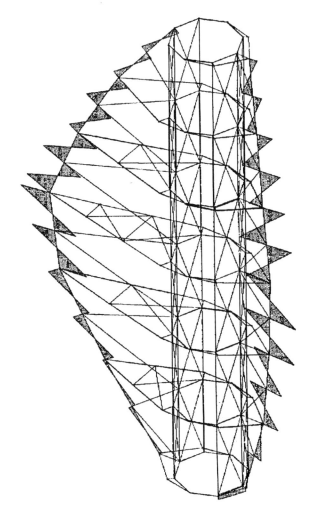

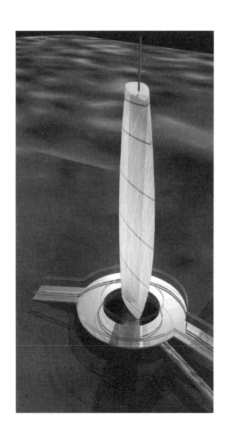

Japan visit: September 1992

In the middle of September 1992 Ron Herron made his penultimate visit to Toyama.

I had a series of meetings to which Tom had to keep driving me. I asked Tom whether we could have the Kurobe meeting at the hotel? So the mayor and the local architects came to the hotel with 26 detail drawings and we met in the restaurant. YKK had apparently said they thought there might be a possibility of using aluminium but in the end, because there would have to be entirely special sections, it would be too expensive. I marked up the drawings in red pen, we had a drink and that was it.

Kurobe started on site on 1 October. The mayor was very eager to have it up before the Christmas snows.

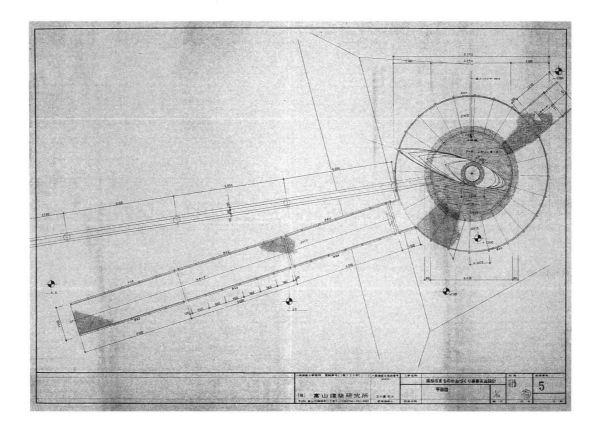

1:200

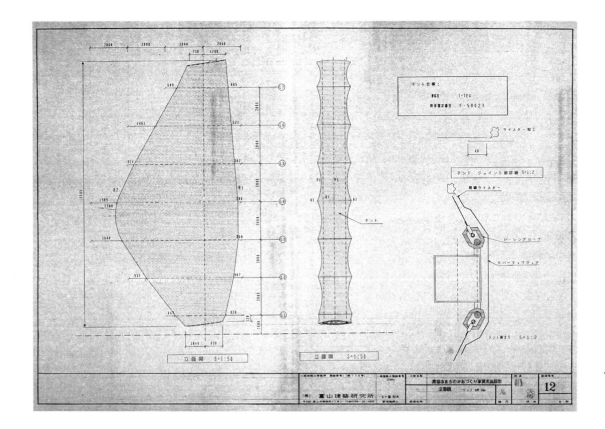

1:200

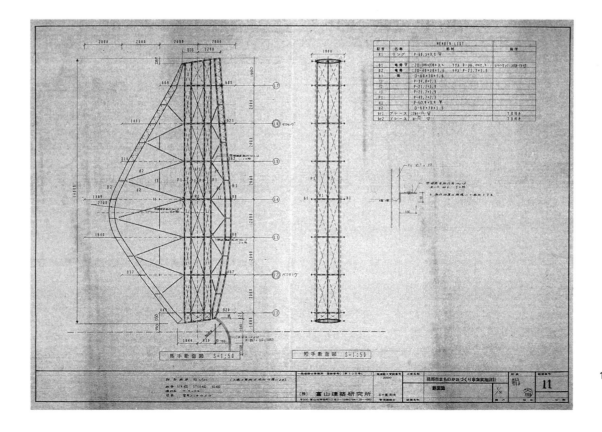

1:200

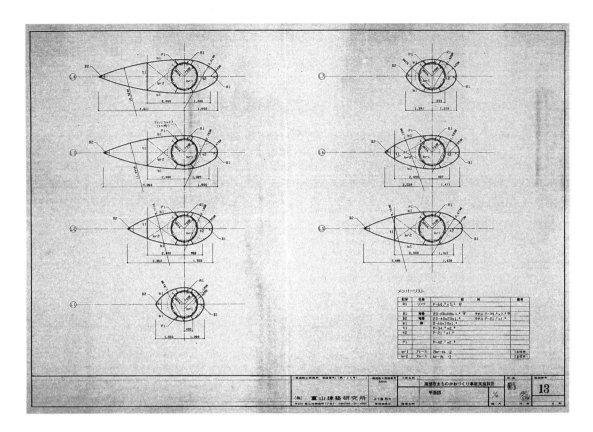

1:200

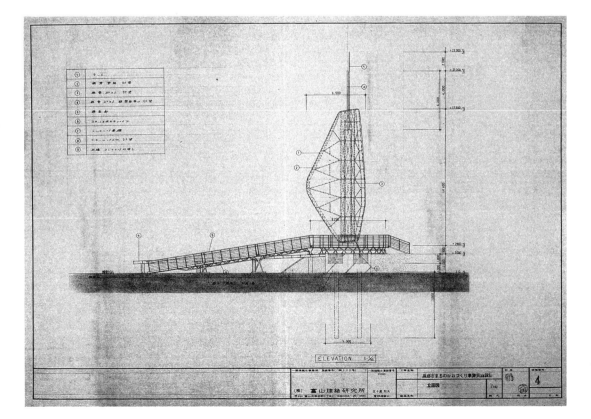

1:400

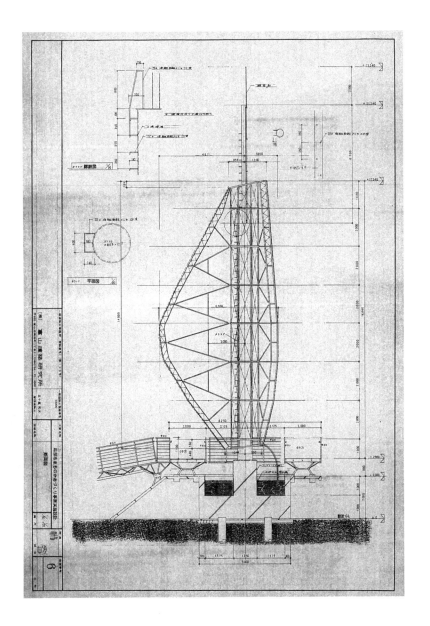

1:200

- TORONTO — 553 M
  T.V. TOWER
- EIFEL 300M
- P.O. TOWER
  LONDON ... 175 M
- SEARS ... 442 M.

500 M
600.

AIR
TRAFFIC.

transportasic' TOWER 88

60 M

30 M

20 M

DESERT.

CITY.

TOWN.

NYC TOWER 1990

kensington 88

canada watar

SPEAK

see

hear

Think

feel

1 2 3

UP

Triangman

Platform (suspended)

Christmas set-up.
RT 1 + 2.

Snowspace
imagination Bldg.
March 87'

Bug Eye

KANTENNE 87'

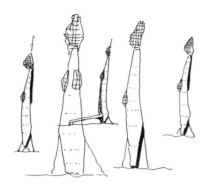

Kurobe

The Kurobe tower represented a different architectural proposition from the Kosugi and Daimon projects. Its proposed function was not particularly clear – there was certainly no need, said the brief, for it to have a utilitarian function. So is not entirely surprising that the Herrons rapidly, nervously, as Herron puts it, went through a series of ideas before coming up with the first wrapped cylinder. Or that they rejected it as soon as they had sent the preliminary sketches off to Japan. The useful part of that exercise was in working out a broad pedestrian strategy for the area and establishing the cherry-blossom plantation as an integral part of the scheme.

Towers have always been tricky for architects. They have to suffer the inevitable old jokes about phallic symbolism from their fellows, taunts about self-aggrandisement and monumentality – and Old-Modernist disapproval about the lack of function. It's not that there aren't towers in the 20th-century architectural canon but the heroic examples such as Mendelsohn's Einstein Tower and the unrealized Tatlin Tower had rooms inside them even if they were either vestigial or suggestions of functioning spaces.

Coincidentally, Herron had been working on a number of tower projects around the same time. One, a vast communications-related tower for the desert, is in his notebook only a few pages before the first Kurobe sketches. And there were other designs from the same time for buildings and exhibition spaces composed of tower-like forms. At a much smaller scale there was a series of tower robots intended for a big atrium which in 1987 Imagination had hoped to lease.

The early Kurobe designs had stairs and for a while, until it was clear they would be too expensive, lifts. The function of these towers was to allow local people to view the surrounding countryside and the last gasp of the cylindrical version had bumps up the shaft serving as intermediate viewing platforms.

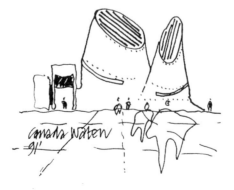

When the Kurobe clients pointed out that they were quite relaxed about the tower not having a function it was a kind of liberation from the European architectural heritage. Its reticence about symbolic representation was anyway quite alien to Japanese culture. Now it was possible to think more clearly about how the work could become a fascinating object and stretch the possibilities as far as structure and the budget would allow. The Herrons are not as a matter of course preoccupied with the inner reaches of symbolism but the brief had talked about the tower somehow responding to the two most prevalent elements: high winds and the water of the adjoining canals and rice fields – and Toyama Bay only a few hundred metres beyond. What had become most intriguing was the idea of making the tower move: not perhaps in the way the robot tower sketches had intimated but according to the prevailing Toyama winds. Here was a tower which would satisfy both cultures: one which for the Japanese carried the symbolism of wind and (after Herron's fast thinking at his presentation meeting) water; and which for the Herrons did something interesting. The Taiyo Tent engineers, at first worried about wracking stresses up the structure and the size of the damping paddle in the pool below, suddenly became serene about everything and, in the great engineering tradition, decided to wait and see what happened when the structure was up. The whole thing had become a modest excursion into the unknown. That's something in the late-20th, regulation-ridden century which architecture and engineering rarely ever get to be.

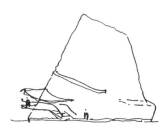

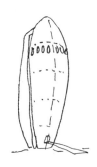

Completed, standing at the end of its triangle of land – even without the cherry-blossom plantation in place, the tower's white sail looks absolutely right. Disturbingly, for an object of such a size, it suddenly moves and the approaching viewer's perception of what it is and what it does becomes uncertain. Close up, for the Western viewer at least, the pool, now probably with only a vestigial paddle in the form of a tube of steel, has the enigmatic quality of a secret commemorative spring.

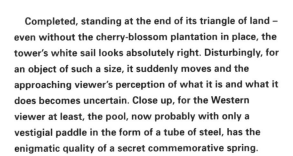

Kensington 88

Montparnasse Tower 88

Daimon

Daimon is a small town up in the hills near Kosugi: mountains in the background, an old shrine in its own grounds nearby. The surrounding hills are studded with flues – the remains of an old roof-tile industry which made mostly black-glazed tiles. There are a few working potteries and a pottery school. The main industry of the town is now electronics.

Every May Daimon puts on a national kite festival: there are permanent bleachers on the gravel bed of the old floodplain where teams from all over Japan fly great house-sized kites in the clear spring air.

The loose brief was to design a bus waiting shelter for around ten people at any one time, and perhaps something else. Herron was given a budget and told that local planning rules allowed him to build on 80 per cent of the site with no particular height restriction.

SITE.

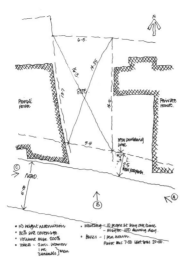

On 31 October 1991, just before Ron Herron was to make his first visit to Japan with preliminary ideas for Kosugi and Kurobe, Tom Heneghan faxed the news that Daimon council wanted to speak with him.

To James Philipps
From Tom Heneghan
31 October 1991

Hello James, etc.

Another project! I mentioned this to Ron earlier as a possibility. There is a town called Daimon (nice name). They want a project. We want Ron to do it. (Sounds simple doesn't it?) We suggested two possible projects. Make a decision? What's 'a decision'??? So the story is that we would like Ron to pop into Daimon and have a look at the possible sites and discuss the possible projects. Anyway this is what we hope to arrange. I emphasize – we hope to arrange.

A meeting was eventually fixed for 13 November when Ron Herron went to have lunch with the mayor of Daimon and talked through the possibilities.
Herron made some rough plan sketches at the meeting and later photographed the site.
   The site is in the main street with electric poles and cables flying around, flanked by two-storey houses. There is a supermarket opposite on the south side of the street. An irregular rectangle between two houses, it is 5.6 metres across the street frontage, around 14 metres deep, widening to 6.5 metres at the back. It later turned out that it would be necessary to allow access to and from the school at the back of the site.

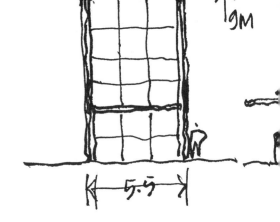

First ideas: 2 November 1991

Back in London, Herron's first idea was to make a permanent exhibition of kites: the idea of the building as a metaphor of kites flying – in a sense a glass non-building in which the architecture was the kites.

If I could have installed an air curtain to act as the enclosure for the slot I would have done it. At the moment that's not technologically possible. We had to have a physical enclosure and that lead to the glass idea.

Ron Herron had decided against early glass proposals for Kosugi by Simon Herron and James Philipps. Here at Daimon it seemed a possibility. They decided on 8–10-metre-high solid flanking walls with glass wrapped around the front, top and back with, perhaps, a mezzanine level inside and shooting-stick-like seating, one of a number of elements which, they hoped, would repeat across the three Japanese schemes.

Because the sides of the site were not parallel, there was the obvious problem of how to configure overhead tracks for the gantry needed to clean the glass. But these were early days for that kind of detail. Anyway, in the background there were lurking alternatives such as cleaning robots and self-cleaning films.

One of the early design conversations went like this:

Andrew: A flock of kites …
Simon: Could they be real kites?
Andrew: So the external canopy is a facsimile of the real kites inside. There's a progression from representation to real which is mixed up with the structure holding the glass up.
Simon: … with the structure supporting the glass as thin as possible.
Ron: There'll be some structure on the roof, but we don't want to clog it up with too much structure.
Andrew: … take it through the structure of the kite?
Simon: That's too literal.
Ron: I think it's a canopy – which has a relationship with the building which we don't want to confuse.
Simon: Need it be a glass thing?
Ron: I think you can put a canopy …

Simon: The relationships are part of the whole thing.
Ron: I think it flies separately as a canopy.
Simon: So there should be a gap.
Ron: But you need a connection.
Simon: I like the existing simple structure.
Ron: The thought I had going home last night was that it should be a kite.
Simon: If it came in and out during different seasons …

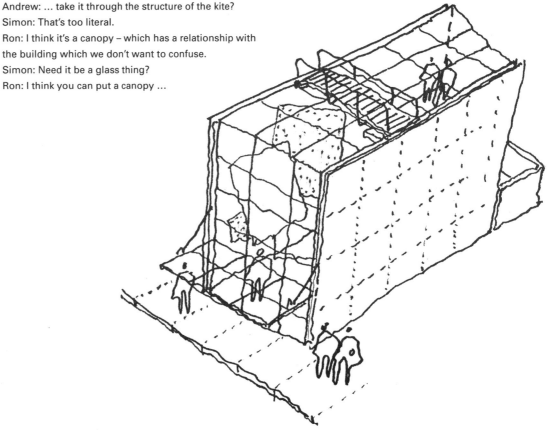

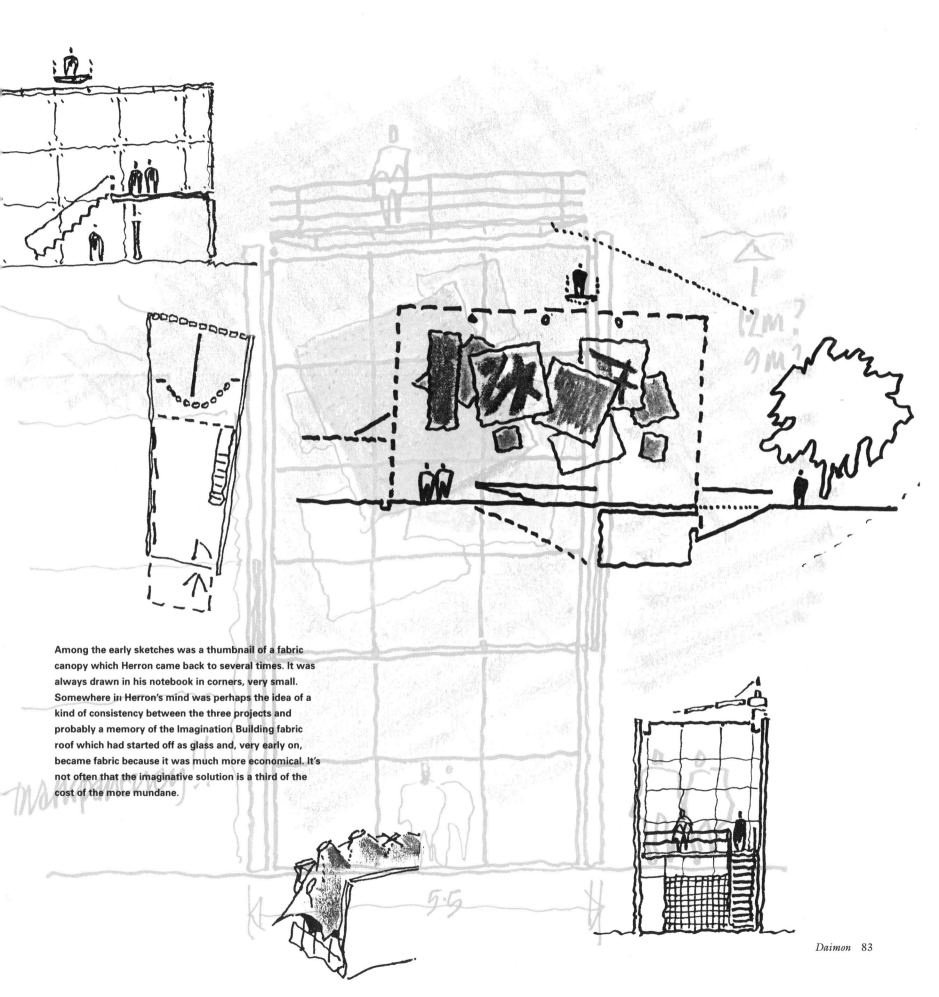

Among the early sketches was a thumbnail of a fabric canopy which Herron came back to several times. It was always drawn in his notebook in corners, very small. Somewhere in Herron's mind was perhaps the idea of a kind of consistency between the three projects and probably a memory of the Imagination Building fabric roof which had started off as glass and, very early on, became fabric because it was much more economical. It's not often that the imaginative solution is a third of the cost of the more mundane.

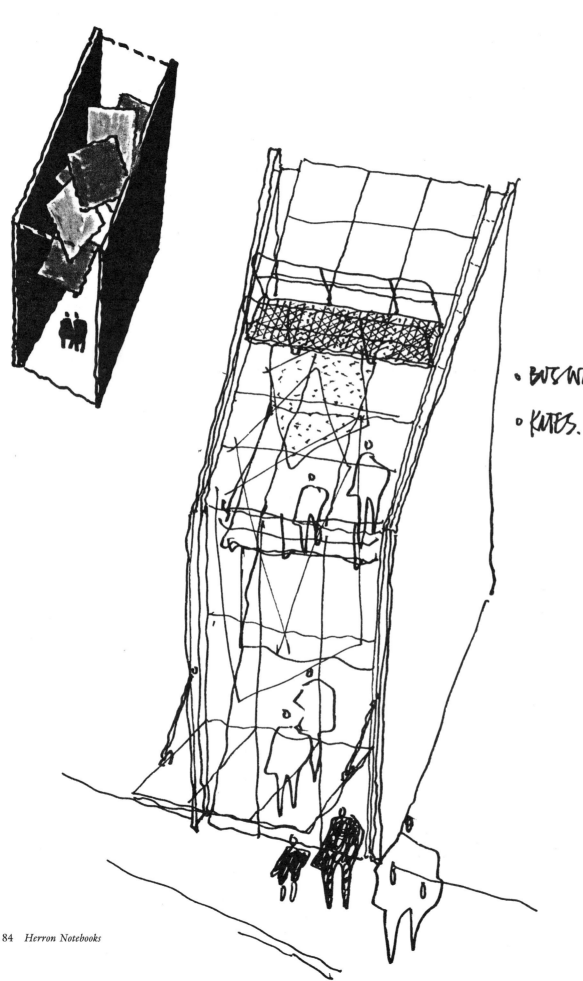

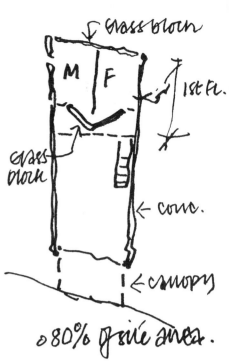

Glass block

M | F

1st Fl.

Glass block

← conc.

← canopy

o 80% of site area.

• BUS WAITING.

• KITES.

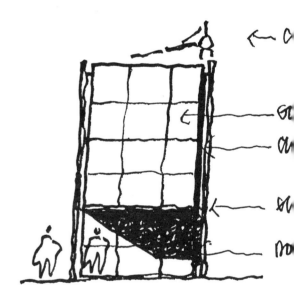

← C

GL

CO

SL

PO

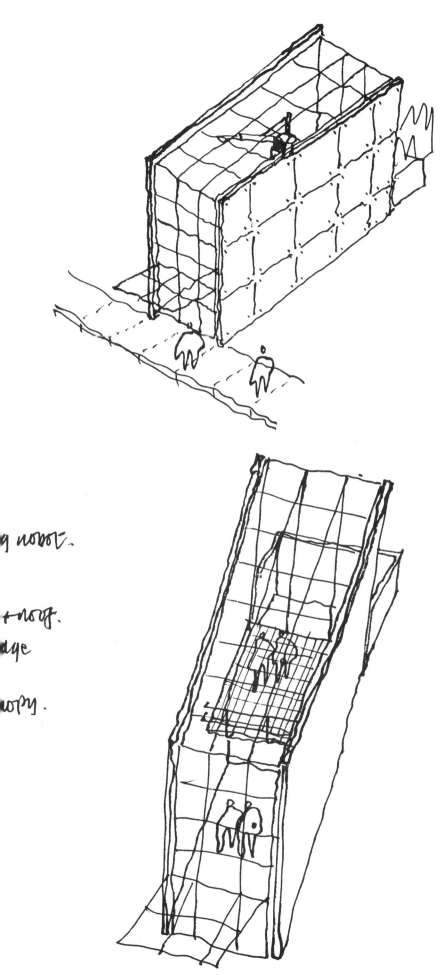

Over the next days the Herrons looked at variations on the glass theme, one with the lavatories under a mezzanine, others with the lavatories underground. In some cases the yard at the back (the 20 per cent of the site which could not be built on) sloped down like a London terrace area to light the underground toilet designs. The idea looked about right but, as he noted in a December sketch, Herron had an uneasy feeling about the cost.

You sneak bits in where you can, often things which on the face of it don't appear to be very interesting. For example, at Daimon it was the roof we were interested in. So you use these things to strengthen an architectural idea. All of the Toyama projects have been more or less like that.

At Daimon the original glass box with the kites was very pure, and I got interested in the idea of how you cleaned the glass and the cleaning robot. It would probably have ended up as a robot crawling over glass.

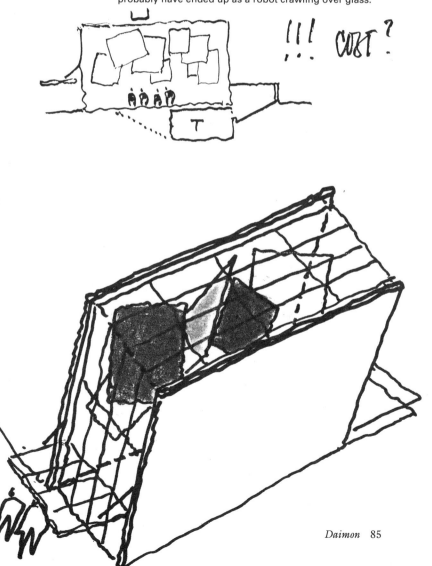

Computer montages of
the early Daimon scheme –
a glass box enclosing a
display of kites – and its
successor – a pink fabric
roof which is itself kite-like.

New directions: January 1992

The Herron design studies continued: looking at the
profiles of the roof, steep or flat humps, humped or
otherwise, front and back overhangs, whether they
should be suspended or strutted, whether the bus
station should be entirely open or have a glass front wall
and whether the rear yard should be enclosed in steel
mesh or concrete.

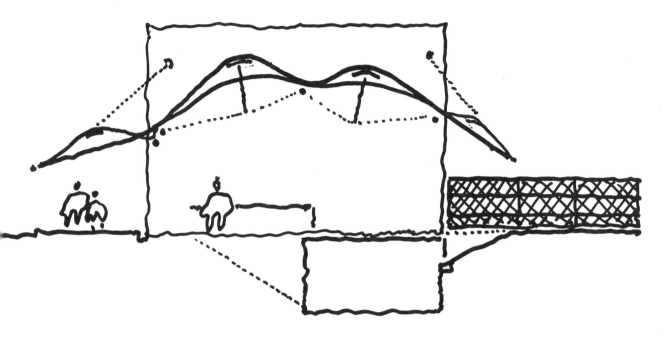

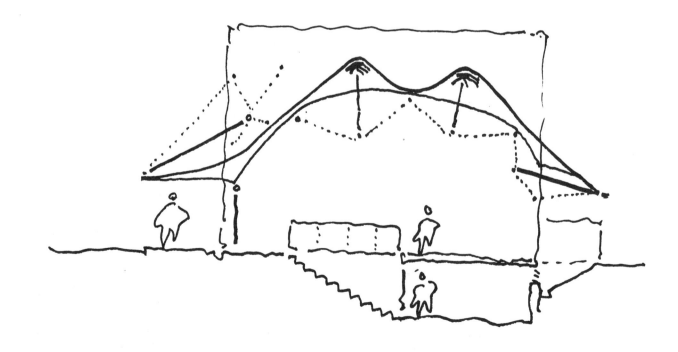

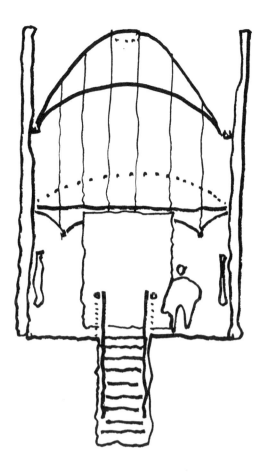

In mid January, unaware of the new direction of the design in London, Suichi Fujie, producer for the whole Machi no Kao project, faxed with some worries about maintaining the glass skin – and the kites. He also suggested that the building need not be airtight.

To Ron Herron
From Suichi Fujie
13 January 1992

Could you please find the following comments:
We would like to support the structurally simple appearance: a strength of contrast between the industrial materials and the kites with their colours visible even in these first sketches. We feel they will provide inspiration and imagination for people waiting for buses.

We have some questions about whether Daimon will be able to maintain a bus stop which is also an exhibition area … We have to try to foresee the future …

So would you please consider opening this space to the air without a perfect roof and to allow for more maintenance-freeness than the present idea. We would also like to ask you to develop the following possibilities: the number of kites exhibited could be decreased or they could be shown in some sort of glass wall or window – or in some other way which is maintenance free.

Suichi Fujie also pointed out that the glazing alone would cost around ¥50 million, the underground lavatories around ¥10 million.

Realizing they hadn't told Japan about the current fabric designs, the Herrons immediately faxed a sketch to Heneghan and noted their astonishment at the cost of the concrete walls. He replied that the high concrete cost was to do with the wall thickness needed for earthquake-proof design. His suggestion was to reduce the height of the walls and make the fabric steeper to shed snow. He cautiously questioned the need to use real kites because the building was itself so very kite-like.

Frankly, your fabric roof sketch has the potential to look more kite-like than a real kite and we can see an argument for suggesting that it is not necessary actually to exhibit kites since the building itself has the character and delicate quality of a kite in flight. In a way the building exaggerates the principle characteristic of the town and becomes the only building in Daimon which expresses, all year, the famous Daimon kite festival which takes place only for a short time … it may not be a tragedy if the building is not full of kites and you can more clearly see the delicacy of the roof.

There were also the problems of local bike gangs, saki-louts, vandalizing anything delicate, and the prohibitive cost of locating the lavatories underground. It would have meant installing an expensive pump to raise waste to the levels of the existing town sewerage system.

Heneghan wrote persuasively, 'If you consider the building to be an enclosure then the presence of a WC box is uncomfortable in the space. But if the scheme is seen more as a roofed and partly walled open space then a WC box is less of an intrusion. Or could the WC be in a fat side wall? Or could it be inside a sculptural staircase leading up to the higher level platform? Or could the WCs be inside an artificial hard landscape rising up from floor level? Or could the side walls move closer together and the WC be accessed from outside one of the long walls so that the WCs are seen as bulges into the interior space? Or. Or. As usual your schemes are far more fun to fantasize about than my own.'

The voice of the experienced Architectural Association tutor is audible here.

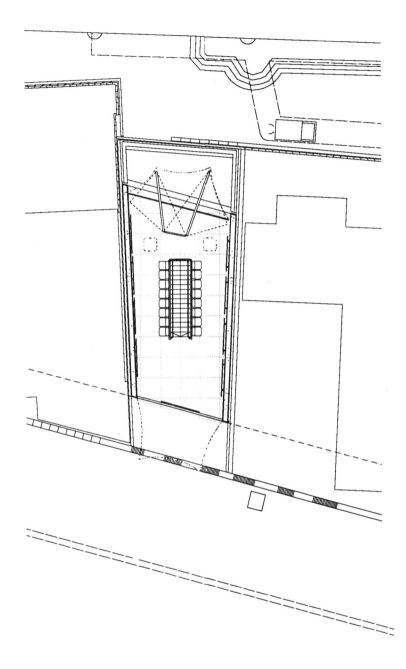

1:200

In late January there was not sufficient time to revise the location of the lavatories before Ron Herron started off for his third visit to Japan. So for the time being they stayed where they were. The Herrons had finally decided to use a two-hump canopy with the front overhang propped down with struts and tension cables from the side walls above and the rear overhang pulled down from below.

On 13 February Herron presented these drawings and the computer models (see overpage) and a model to Daimon council.

The new design got a good reception.

They hadn't seen the fabric version before this but here they had the model in their hands. The mayor was very amused by the pink tent and liked the idea of the expression of the kite form as a kind of container in the high street which might spark off more ideas for the rest of the town.

He also loved the computer images and I offered to give a talk to students (it's a robot-making town) about robots in architecture.

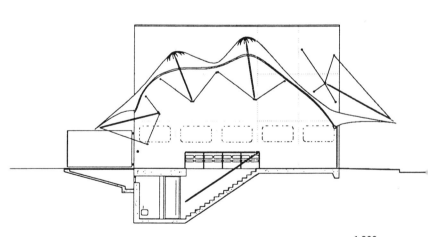

1:200

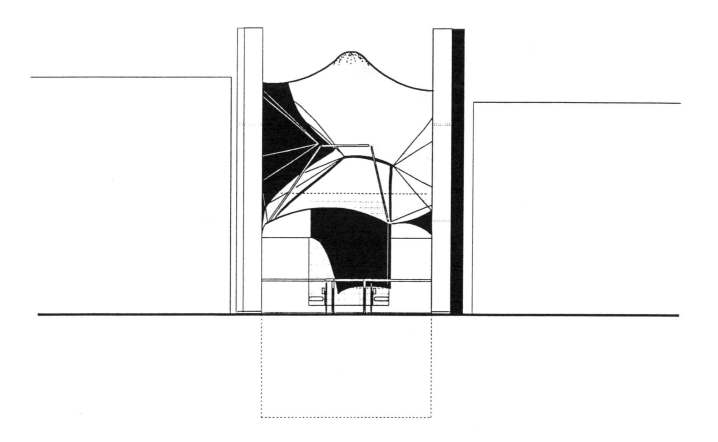

1:100

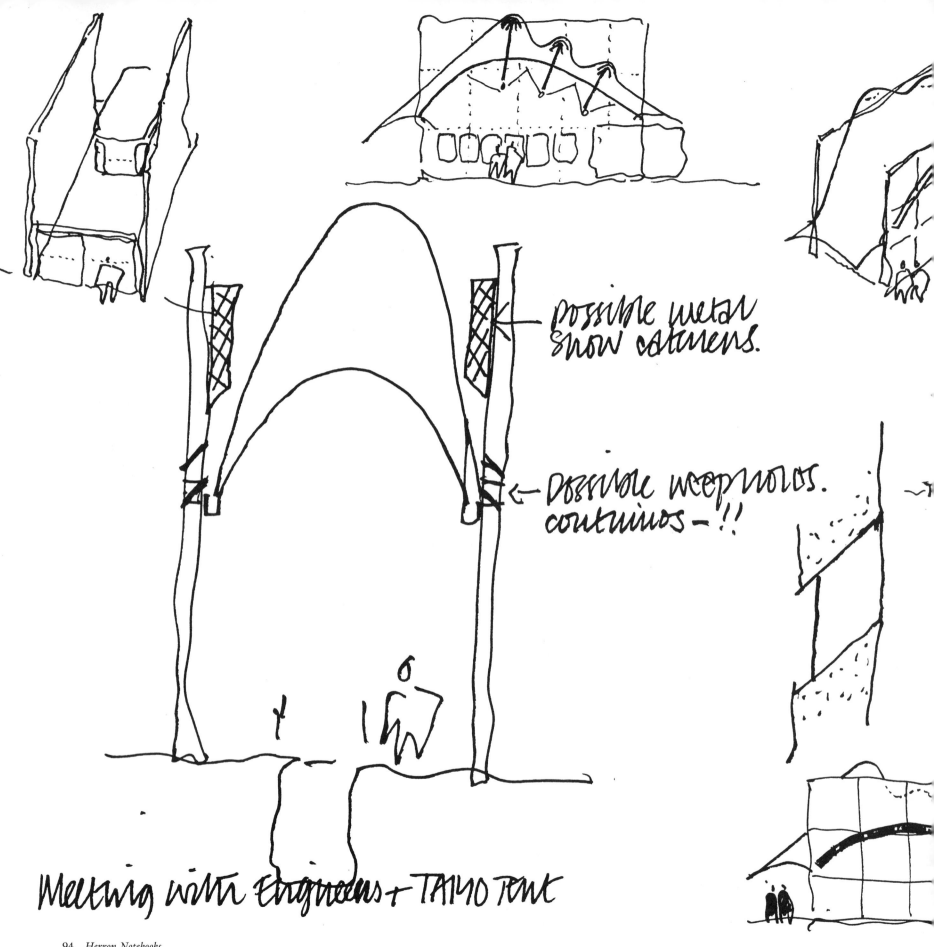

possible metal
snow catchers.

← possible weepholes.
continuos – !!

Meeting with Engineers + TAIYO Tent

In Daimon Ron Herron had a meeting with the local architect, Shigeo Yoshida of Yoshida Kenchiku Jimsho, and talked about snow loads. Shigeo Yoshida asked for more than the proposed two bumps in the canopy and steeper dips in the fabric to reduce spans and to shed snow. Herron had been intrigued with the idea of passers-by being showered with drifting snow. The Taiyo Tent engineers, with whom he was also talking, pointed out that snowfalls in Daimon were very heavy and a roof shedding a big load could kill people. In any case, with three humps the allowable snow loads could be significantly reduced and the supporting structure made lighter. Herron abandoned the two-bump idea but promised to send a kite from Neal Street in London and the Taiyo engineers promised to send fabric samples.

The walls would also have to be reduced in height for cost reasons already outlined by Heneghan in January. This offered the possibility of having the top humps rising above the height of the flank walls.

There was also the possibility of snow catchers attached along the upper inside faces of the flank walls with holes to shed the snow through the walls. And then it occurred to Herron that the snow could be drained by a long curving slit cut in the flanking walls, following the profile of the outer edges of the canopy. He sketched out the ideas in the meetings and thought more about them in his hotel room.

Back in Kosugi, work on the station canopy had just started on site.

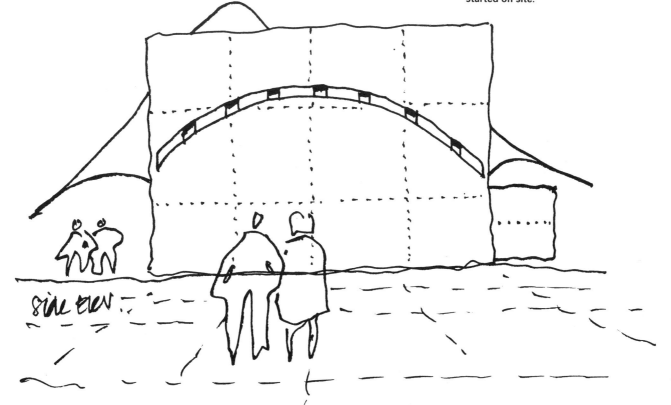

SIDE ELEV

Ceramics: March 1992

Daimon town council had asked if Herron could incorporate something to do with their tile industry – beautiful jet-black and deep blue ceramics. He had always wanted to do something like this since seeing Le Corbusier's doors at Ronchamp. His hope was that the local ceramic industry could produce tiles of, say, a metre or half a metre square but he wasn't sure. The local tiles, beautifully glazed in intense colours, were curved roof tiles of relatively small size.

In mid April Heneghan asked whether it would be possible to achieve the panels in any other way 'without incurring a budget crisis; i.e. stove enamelling, etc.'

In February the mayor took me to look at the local ceramic education centre – a kiln, workshop and gallery and teaching place. He asked if it would be possible somehow to incorporate tiles into the design. I thought he meant roof tiles. I laughed, but it turned out he meant using tiles made from the local clay and glazed there.

That sounded interesting.

The idea I had was to use them for the faces of the lavatories, building up an image which could be cast in sections and fired and put together on the wall. Because of the town's association with kites, we could use a design which evoked them. So the designs developed as a strong black image which I began to blow up so it looked less and less like a kite. I got quite into this. Once you start to blow the image up it becomes increasingly abstract – a bit like Patrick Caulfield's early work.

The two toilet blocks were rather like assemblages with sliding doors and panel-like fronts and backs. When they became a single block the idea wasn't appropriate any more. I had sent some prints to Tom and eventually he faxed that we couldn't do it.

It's one of those things you always wanted to do: you'd like the freedom to do something without regulations and constraints – purely as an object. Usually you don't because you're not an artist. But if you can clock it into the building …

I tried to do it in the Imagination Building with a big pivot door dividing the reception area from the front desk: an abstract work made up of stove-enamelled pieces. But they didn't want to split the space.

I could have pushed Daimon but it now had no real relevance. I'd probably be arguing against it now.

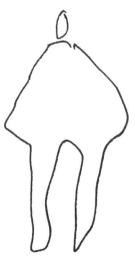

The slot and the wrapping: April–May 1992

In early April, residents living around the site protested that they did not want <u>any</u> building there which might encourage kids to hang out and make noise late at night. They had no particular legal rights but, at the time, it seemed that they needed to be given an opportunity to be persuaded. If this turned out to be a protracted political problem the fabric could no longer be attached to the Kosugi order and that would mean paying a lot more for it.

Around the same time more details emerged. Walls would have to be 500 mm from the boundaries. That presented difficulties in fitting in the toilets, now at ground level, and a passageway between. Because the bus station would be used occasionally as a route for kids from the school at the rear, it was suggested that toilet walls face outward away from the central route. However, because of the reduced internal width, the town council would accept only one WC for each sex, and a urinal. It was important with crouch lavatories (which were being used here) to position toilet-roll holders on the left-hand side wall – and because the space outside was a waiting space the doors had to be sound proofed.

Heneghan suggested that it might be politic to allow the neighbouring buildings more light in some way.

On 8 May Tom Heneghan sent a detailed fax.

To Ron Herron
From Tom Heneghan
8 May 1991

We had a meeting with Taiyo yesterday. It emerged that we
would need downpipes at the end of each gutter to prevent
a deluge falling off the roof at the corners. The walls are
300 mm thick and it may, but also may not, be possible to
recess the downpipes in the thickness of the wall with the
pipes flush with one surface of the wall. Another option is to
hide the downpipes in framing which supports the edges of
the glazed screen and the mesh tower. Another option is to
put the downpipes on the outside of the concrete walls
However, our engineer is suggesting a return to an option
he discussed with Ron: cutting a curved slot in each wall
and allowing rain and, more importantly, snow to fall
outside the building but with no downpipes. To prevent
snow building up against the exterior of the neighbouring
buildings he suggests a mesh cage to retain the snow within
the site boundaries. I sketch this on the attached sheet
where I have suggested extending the rear mesh cage along
the sides of the walls with horizontal spacers as supports …

**Tom Heneghan's idea was fascinating, not least because
he had provided the Herrons with a functional reason for
wrapping the whole building with mesh. Heneghan well
understood Ron Herron's long-standing fascination with
the concept of wrapping and they had recently discussed
it on both the Kosugi and Kurobe projects. The day they
received the fax, the Herrons sketched out variants on
the curving slot idea, in some cases with a low concrete
wall serving as a boundary marker at the rear but with
the enclosing open mesh wrap.**

Ten days later there came a fax from Heneghan.

To Simon Herron
From Tom Heneghan
18 May 1992

We have now had comments from the Town on the mesh
option. They say that if we have mesh it must be 500 mm
from the boundary – moving the walls in more. We imagine
that would be a problem. Your local architect therefore
believes that it will be better to have water sprays set into
the tops of the walls which will dissolve snow. We will,
however, need downpipes at front and back.

**The boundary walls had been lowered to 17.5 metres and
pulled in 500 mm at each side. Pulling them in another
metre would make everything very squashed. The
Herrons decided to abandon the wrapping idea
immediately and think about a way of draining the water
more simply.**

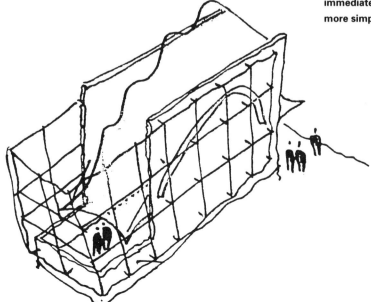

The umbrellas: June 1992

Progress on the Daimon design had slowed down, largely because of the local political difficulties. The Herrons, slightly uneasy, sat tight until, with the completion and opening of the Kosugi project, Tom Heneghan sent a fax.

To Simon Herron
From Tom Heneghan
1 June 1992

First the good news: the mayor of Daimon has been to see Kosugi, thinks it is fantastic and wants his NOW! ... Bad news: I am worried that you won't be happy with the fabric over the umbrellas. The fabric becomes faceted between the fingers of the umbrella heads and is not a smooth curve. Perhaps you have anticipated this and I am worrying over nothing ... Maybe you will want to consider this in the design of the Daimon umbrella heads.

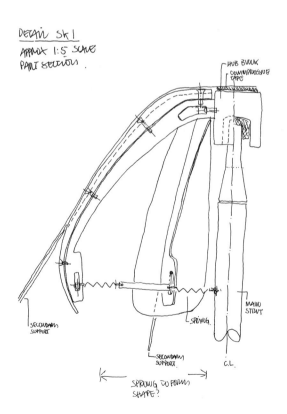

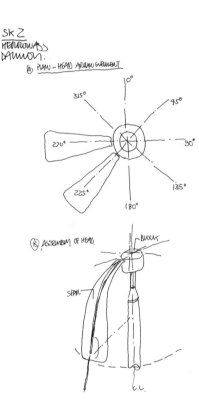

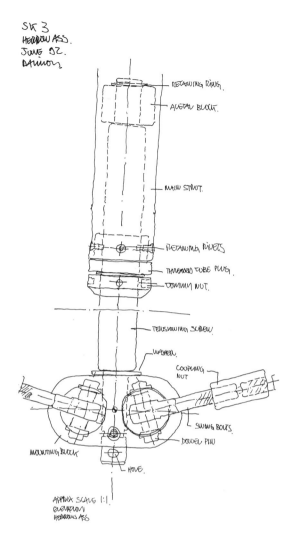

Despite the slowdown, Taiyo Tent's engineers had been working on various configurations of the roof structure, with faxes going backwards and forwards between Tokyo and London. It was now becoming urgent to have the building complete before the middle of November when the first serious snows fell. Heneghan's faxes, alternating with Kazuhiro Ando's, became more and more desperate.

On 9 June Simon Herron sent details of the umbrellas – similar at the base of the push-ups to those designed by John Randall at the Imagination Building but with broad 'paddles' in place of the ribs to reduce the tendency of the fabric to ridge around them.

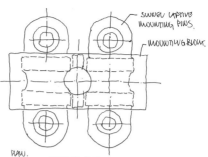

SWIVEL CAPTIVE
MOUNTING PINS.

MOUNTING BLOCK.

PLAN.
TOP VIEW MOUNTING BLOCK
ALL HOLES TO BE REAMED + DEBURRED.
(mounting block)

APPROX SCALE 1:1. SK4.
HEDRON ACS.

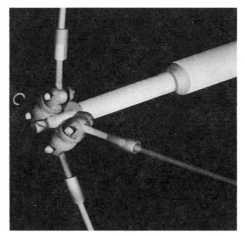

JOINT + PUSH UP MAIN SHAFT
→ PRINCIPLE OF 'MOBILE JOINTS'
SCOTE STREET
SK5

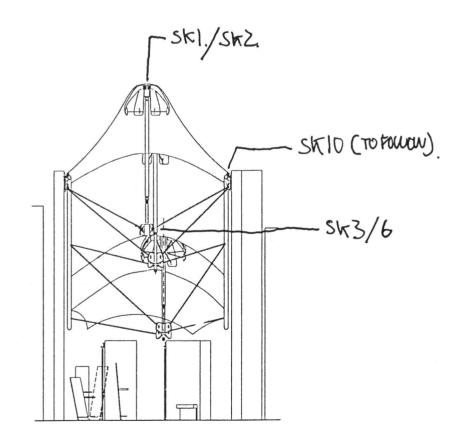

SK1./SK2.

SK10 (TO FOLLOW).

SK3/6

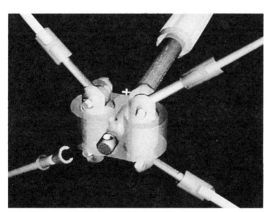

DAIMON → MODULE OF JOINT AT BOTTOM OF FABRIC PUSH UP
'STORE STREET' PRINCIPLE.
SK 6

Engineering by fax: July 1992

The final configuration of the roof had four steep humps, three of them rising above the flank walls and the fourth sloping out over the street. The Taiyo Tent engineers had been grappling with the calculations and resolving the forces as elegantly as possible. Finally they made a graceful gesture.

To Simon Herron
From Tom Heneghan
2 July 1991

Taiyo have asked for permission to use YOUR structural system … The reason is that they feel your system is much superior to their own ideas which they had been advancing as an exercise.

So – can they build your design? Funny question!

A fortnight later Kazuhiro Ando and the Urban Factory engineer had held a meeting with Taiyo Tent about progress on Daimon. Ando faxed their revised detail drawings for approval. As they came out of the fax machine, the reduced drawings looked remarkable and full of detailed information. The Herrons' main concern was whether they looked right – and the pointed umbrellas were not quite the thing. Following this, questions and arguments and alternatives and revisions flowed by fax between London and Tokyo.

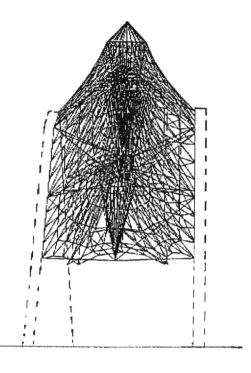

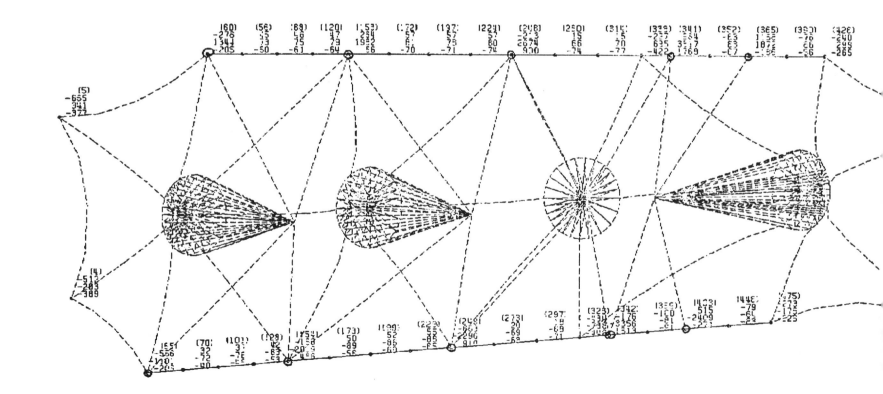

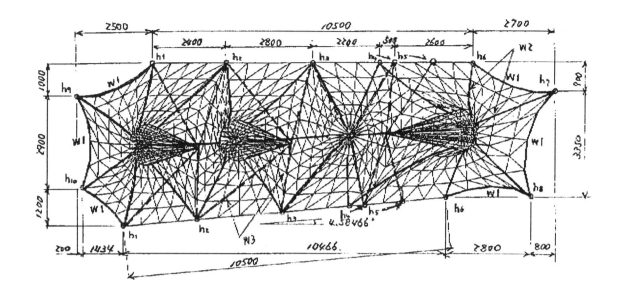

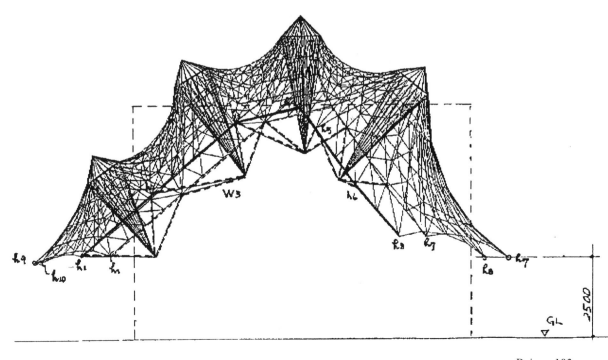

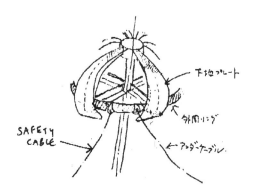

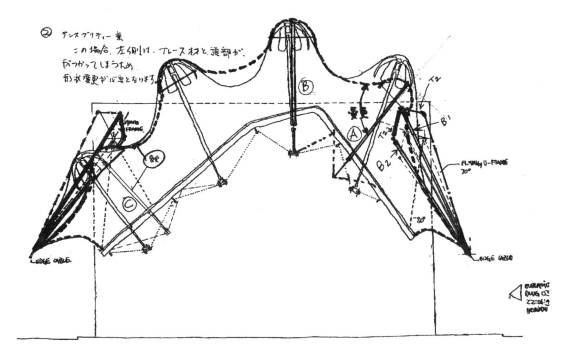

Final structural details: August 1992

Between June and September a number of small changes had been agreed: the lavatory block would not need a urinal although a small storeroom was needed between both booths.

The Town suddenly decided that a glass wall across the back of the shelter would be necessary. Simon Herron was reluctant because he had been led to believe that the prevailing wind was from the street side.

But, as Tom Heneghan pointed out, 'The front and rear glass walls are needed to keep out rain, but they are also needed to reduce wind penetration and its uplift on the fabric roof. It was calculated that if there were no rear glass wall the hold-down anchors in the concrete walls would each have to resist an uplift of 16 tonnes.'

With the new ruling about the toilets it was possible to combine them as one form – which the Herrons then decided to push half way through the new glass wall.

At the same time Simon Herron sent the Toyama engineers a number of sketches to clarify the detailing of the gutter and the method of tying the fabric to the side walls – using a 100 mm tube cranked to follow the edge profile of the roof. Herron asked whether it would be possible to combine the anchorages for the cables supporting the umbrella push-up rods with supports for the gutter.

To Simon Herron
From Tom Heneghan
3 August 1991

This is Taiyo's hybrid of your scheme and their scheme and is the only way they can achieve your preferred image.

The heavy dotted line shows Taiyo's suggested profile. The main alteration is the rotation of props A and B so they are at right angles to the force of the tent to impose even tension on the fabric. The movement of prop C is so that the fabric does not clash with the external flying frame. One valley is slightly shallower to even the tension in the fabric.

Due to the tension in the fabric, the umbrellas will need a ring to maintain the position of the wings (leaves, flaps?). The fabric tension will be too high to be resisted by springs. The ring is also used for the attachment of the safety cables.

They are still working on the gutter. The material will be steel. Stainless would be nice but cost may mean painted. Colour? Now, maybe you have heard this somewhere before, but your decisions on these and all the other matters are urgent. I cannot stress enough how urgent. As I mentioned before, the Mayor wants his building NOW and we must complete the building before the snow starts to fall in mid November.

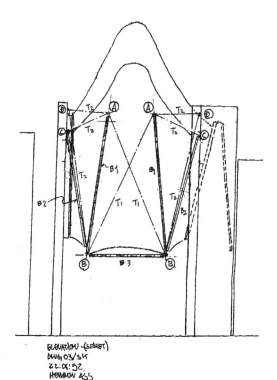

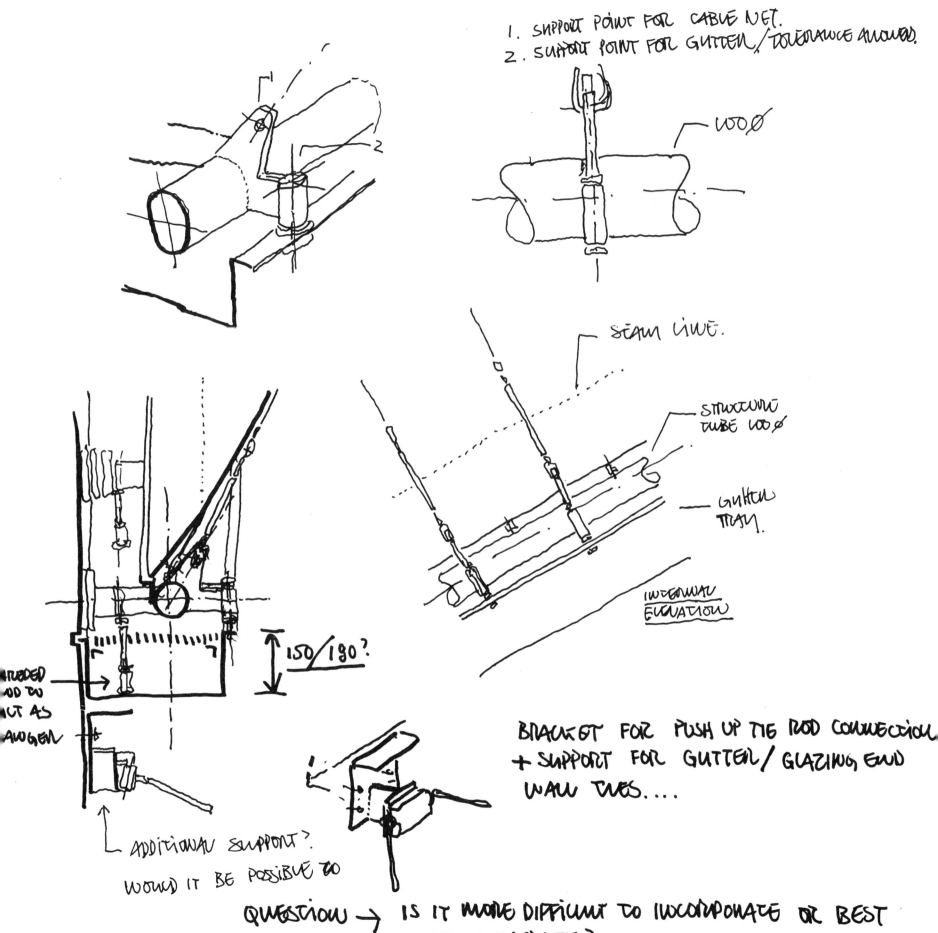

1. SUPPORT POINT FOR CABLE NET.
2. SUPPORT POINT FOR GUTTER / TOLERANCE ALLOWED.

100 ∅

SEAM LINE.

STRUCTURE TUBE 100 ∅

GUTTER TRAY.

INTERNAL ELEVATION

150/180?

EXTRUDED ROD TO ACT AS ANGLED

ADDITIONAL SUPPORT?

WOULD IT BE POSSIBLE TO

BRACKET FOR PUSH UP TIE ROD CONNECTION
+ SUPPORT FOR GUTTER / GLAZING END
WALL TIES....

QUESTION → IS IT MORE DIFFICULT TO INCORPORATE OR BEST
KEPT SEPERATE?

Seating: September 1992

The Urban Factory had been asking about designs for more details including seating. Simon Herron had played around with large, fixed leaning seats but when he went on holiday he had not resolved the final designs. With Daimon in a serious hurry, Ron Herron reworked these designs in a different way.

To Tom Heneghan
From Ron Herron
4 September 1992

Dear Tom
Herewith a sketch (very rough) of possible Kosugi/Daimon seat – leaning seat.

   Not sure about galvanizing + painting, maybe only galvanized … Hopefully they will be scattered facing every which way. It would be good if the 'leg' tubes were thinner (20 mm?) – needs a bit of an engineer's eye over it …

P.S. Maybe we could get a rough version made up.

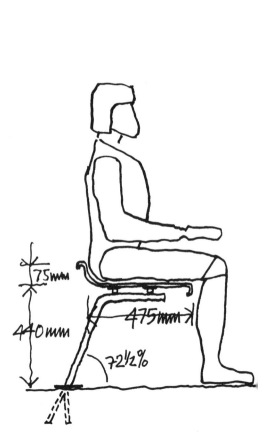

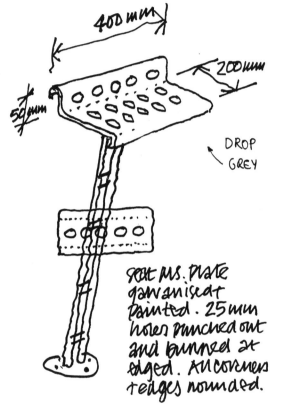

400 mm

200 mm

50 mm

DROP GREY

seat M.S. plate galvanised painted. 25mm holes punched out and burned at edged. All corners redges rounded.

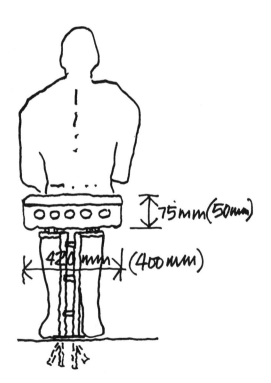

75 mm (50 mm)

420 mm (400 mm)

The seats we have designed will probably be used at Daimon because that was part of the brief. I thought Simon's design was too much of a self-conscious object which needed a much more powerful space, so they've turned out more like shooting sticks in three heights, scattered around randomly in this space of two simple walls and an astonishing pink roof.
I suggested they should be made up in welded galvanized steel by a local blacksmith.

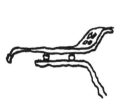

75 mm

440 mm

475 mm

72½%

At his September meeting with the Daimon engineers, the local architects and the Town Council, Ron Herron settled the final design details.

DAIMON. 19.9.92. @ Daimon.

① reduce mesh wall to 2.00 high approx...... make 2m concrete wall with gate.

② reduce main wall height by 500 mm. ....
OK.
asked Taiyo to recalculte gutter and fixings
o Fabric profile stays.

③ lock backdoors. — mean glass not automatic.

④ Water spray (for snow) on top of wall to get rid of snow from gutter

⑤ Fire alarm/bell position .... panic button. cast into wall/above in wall.

⑥ Toilets — separate Male + female as sketch.

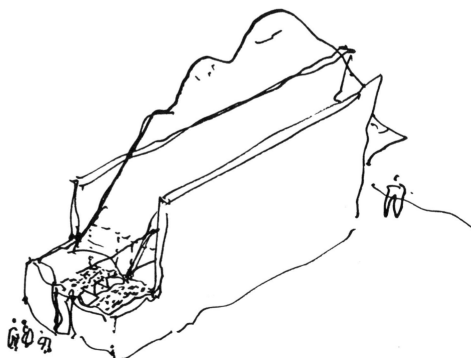

The final scheme: December 1992

The scheme sent to Daimon for final planning approval
had abandoned the mesh in favour of the water spray
along the tops of the walls originally proposed, with
downpipes on the outside faces of the flank walls. Wall
heights were reduced by 500 mm and the staggered
2-metre walls at the rear now enclosed a small garden –
and the profiles of the humps adjusted to throw snow off
every part of the roof. The lavatories, now a single block,
pushed through the new rear glass wall.

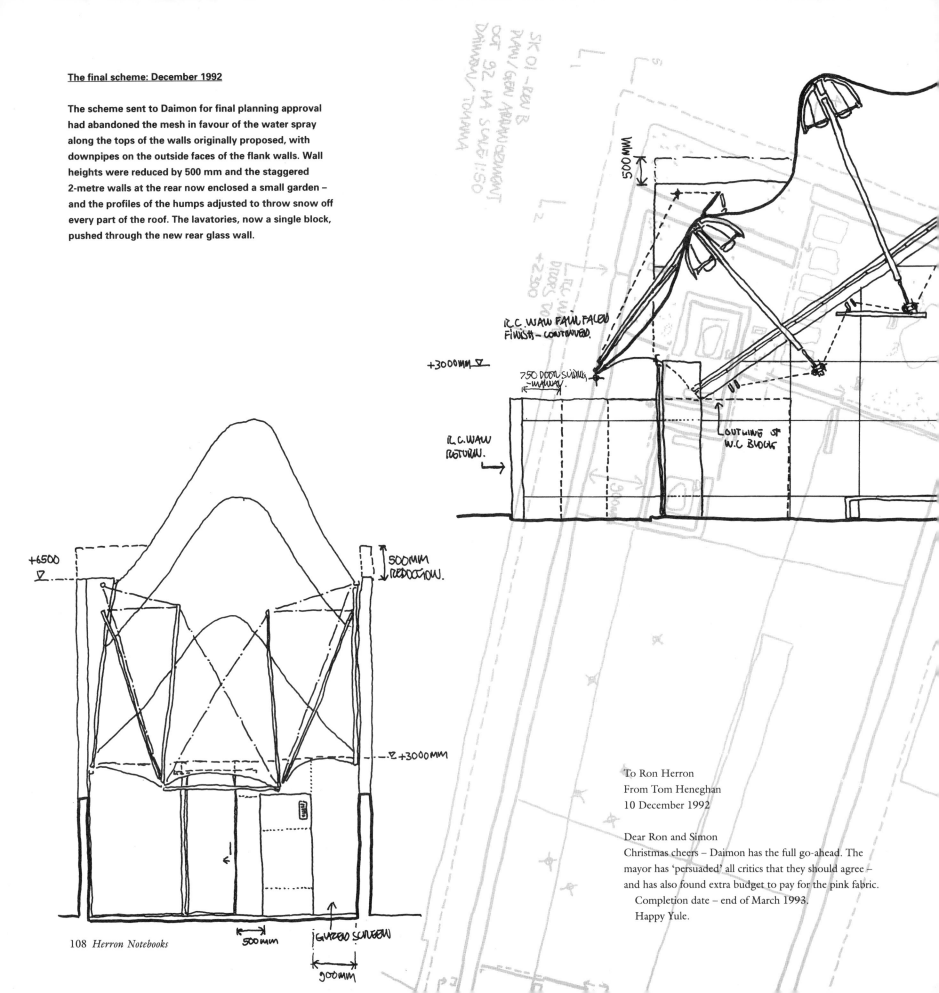

SK 01 – REV B
PLAN / GEN ARRANGEMENT
OCT 92 HA SCALE 1:50
DAIMON / TOKAWA

500 MM

RC WALL FAIR FACED
FINISH – CONTOURED.

+3000MM ▽

750 DOOR SLIDING
– midway.

OUTLINE OF
W.C BLOCK

RC. WALL
RETURN.

+6500
▽

500MM
REDUCTION.

▽ +3000MM

500mm

900mm

GLAZED SCREEN

To Ron Herron
From Tom Heneghan
10 December 1992

Dear Ron and Simon
Christmas cheers – Daimon has the full go-ahead. The
mayor has 'persuaded' all critics that they should agree –
and has also found extra budget to pay for the pink fabric.
Completion date – end of March 1993.
Happy Yule.

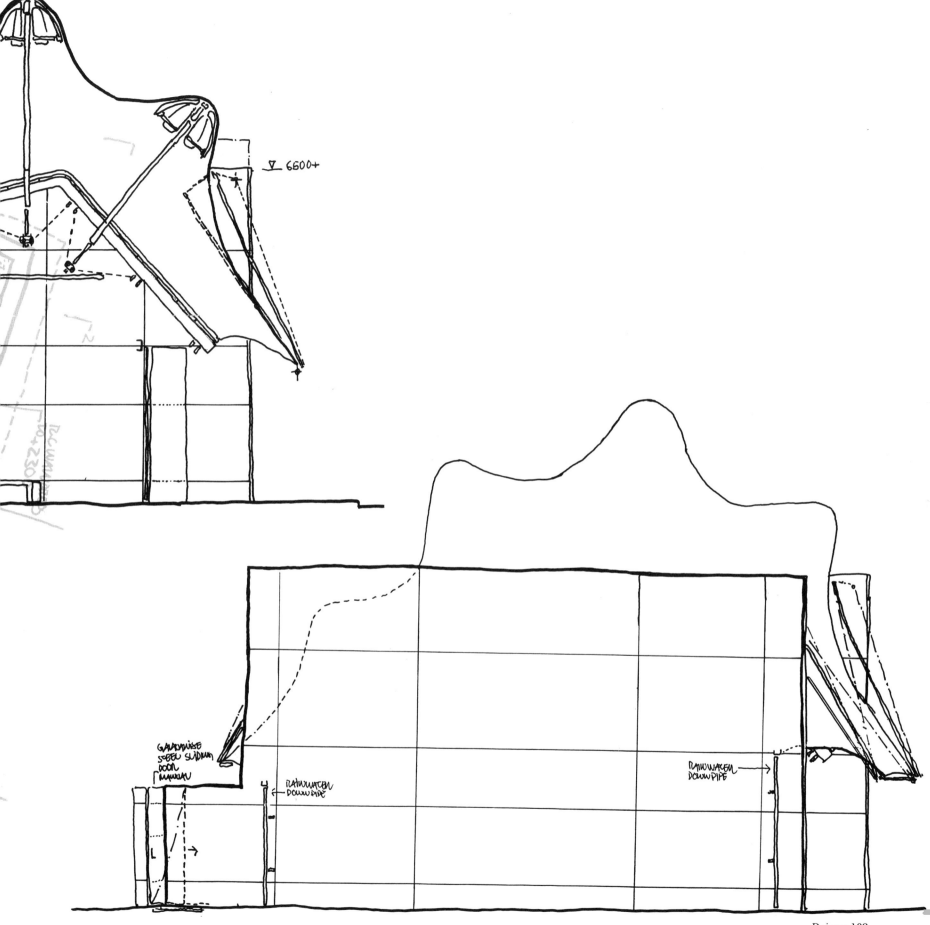

▽ 6500+

GALVANISED
STEEL SLIDING
DOOR
MARKED

RAINWATER
DOWN PIPE

RAINWATER
DOWN PIPE

L

On site: Late February 1993

In mid February 1993 the local architects had sent the Herrons snapshots of the first excavations. Then came the final set of detailed drawings. Daimon council had asked for one of the toilets to be for disabled people and because time was very short they had attached it to the side wall. Ron Herron's choice of unframed toughened glass was too expensive and the local architects had adopted a conventional solution.
Herron immediately faxed a carefully restrained note and a series of sketches explaining how he wanted the design to go.

To Kazuhiro Ando
From Ron Herron
22 February 1993

Dear Ando-san
Just received Daimon drawings and return herewith my comments.

It's very important that they understand what we are trying to do:
(a) The toilets must be free of side walls.
(b) The entrance is like a porch – i.e. a Le Corbusier quote – and has concrete sides and top.
(c) Glazing should not have an intermediate rail – i.e. door and glazing should be full height. (Are the doors still magic-eye operated?)
(d) Colour – all metalwork grey as at Kosugi; the only colour apart from the pink roof will be inside toilets! To be decided.
(e) Light fittings – too many types.
I hope you can deal with this as it could be a disaster.
Kurobe looks fantastic.
From worried of London
Ron

Heneghan replied, setting out the background and promising a rapid response.

To Ron Herron
From Tom Heneghan and Kazuhiro Ando
24 February 1993

Dear Ron
There are a few changes the Town would like. These are the result of three problems: (a) getting agreements from neighbours (including the school); (b) Daimon is not as wealthy as Kosugi – and doesn't have many maintenance staff; (c) the budget is tight.
To answer the questions in your fax:
(a) the local architects will discuss this again with the mayor – who personally supports your plan but must persuade the Council. The local architects will re-present a plan based on your drawing but with the box off-centre – this is to allow a minimum 1200 mm access to the disabled toilet and increase the through-route width to 1500 mm. The Council wants the through-route to be more emphasized than the toilet access.
(b) Porch – OK (but please check height on new drawings when they arrive – see comment below on cost).
(c) No magic eye (cost) but automatic locking at night. Because of budget they cannot use toughened glass, only float glass which will not be thick and will need a steel frame …
(d) Metalwork will be in grey. However, Daimon cannot afford maintenance very often and the Council wants to TILE the inside of the toilets – any colour you wish. Hmm.
(e) Lights will be as you require. Photos of fittings will be sent.
Now, because of neighbours and the school, the back wall cannot be concrete but must be mesh – vertical and horizontal weave.

There is need for natural light to enter the toilets. Local architects suggest using glass blocks on the side walls of the WC … Maybe a rooflight.

So generally there are some cost problems which will limit the elegance of the glazing. The local architects understand what you are seeking and will revise the drawings … We imagine the biggest problem will be the detailing of the glass framing, etc., which will probably be fairly chunky to deal with earthquake, in float glass.

You can probably tell from my dull tone that I'm doing my office accounts and my brain cells are self-destructing.

Mulling over Heneghan's fax, Herron realized that if the float glass was going to need earthquake-proof framing the design should be changed so that the glazing was deliberate, and, remembering Kosugi, that if it was decided to use glass blocks they should form a single plane across the back of the widened toilet block – with steel re-entrant corners.

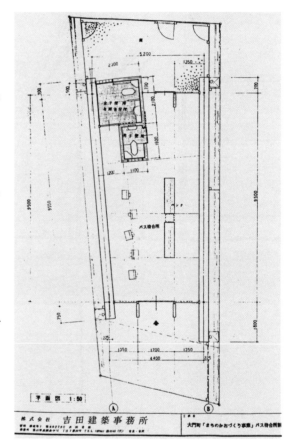

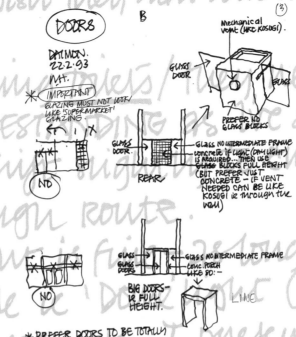

DOORS

DAIMON.
22.2.93
NH.

* IMPORTANT
GLAZING MUST NOT LOOK
LIKE 'SUPERMARKET'
GLAZING.

NO

REAR

Mechanical
vent (like KOSUGI).

GLASS
DOOR

GLASS

PREFER NO
GLASS BLOCKS

GLASS NO INTERMEDIATE FRAME
CONCRETE IF LIGHT (DAY LIGHT)
IS REQUIRED... THEN USE
GLASS BLOCKS FULL HEIGHT
(BUT PREFER JUST
CONCRETE - IF VENT
NEEDED CAN BE LIKE
KOSUGI ie THROUGH THE
WALL)

GLASS
GLASS
DOORS

GLASS NO INTERMEDIATE FRAME
CONC. PORCH
LIKE SO :-

NO

BIG DOORS -
ie FULL
HEIGHT.

LINE

* PREFER DOORS TO BE TOTALLY
  GLASS.
* IF NOT - MUST BE FULL HEIGHT.
* HANDLES - I WANT TO SEE PICTURE (SAMPLE).

To Tom Heneghan
From Ron Herron
26 February 1993

Got your fax re changes – I understand the problem … and
wish they had told me at the time!!

But – regarding the toilets, they MUST be FREE-
STANDING as I've shown – they can shift slightly to
emphasize the through route.

Rooflight is fine – as long as it's kept simple, i.e. a
domelight (flattish).

If glass blocks, I prefer them to be on the main façade and
in a steel frame as at Kosugi (see sketch).

Regarding GLAZING. OK, but must keep glazing bars as
slim as possible and MUST break down glazing as shown –
i.e. DELIBERATELY.

DOOR handles – I want to see!

Regarding PORCH, I haven't had new drawings but I
don't see any problem – it won't make any sense without a
top. Note that glazing runs on the inside (see sketch).

P.S. Regarding tiling in toilet – OK; I would like the same
tiles on walls and floor (at least same colour) but would like
very bright ELECTRIC blue (i.e. like the blue we saw on
the [Daimon] roofing tiles). The door to toilets (+ frames)
to be painted the same blue (inside and out). The ceiling
also to be painted, but PINK to match fabric.

As this book went to press in late April 1993,
Daimon's concrete retaining walls had finally been
built and the fabric roof was about to be erected.

LIGHTING.

SEEMS VERY MESSY - TOO MANY
DIFFERENT FITTINGS.
NEED TO SEE SAMPLES (PICTURES)
OF FITTING.
LIGHT FITTING SHOULD BE 'TOUGH'
- INDUSTRIAL NOT 'PRETTY' AND
DOMESTIC.
REDUCE TYPES.

* ASSUME TYPE ② ARE IN FLOOR?
WHICH IS FINE BUT THEY SHOULD
RUN LIKE SO →

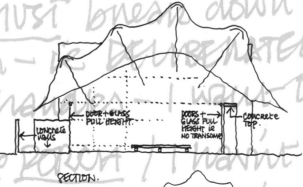

DOOR + GLASS
FULL HEIGHT.

CONCRETE
WALLS

DOORS +
GLASS FULL
HEIGHT ie
NO TRANSOME

CONCRETE
TOP

SECTION.

DAIMON
NH. 22.2.93'.

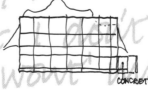

CONCRETE.

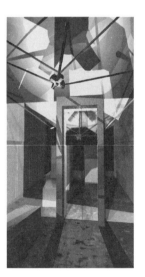

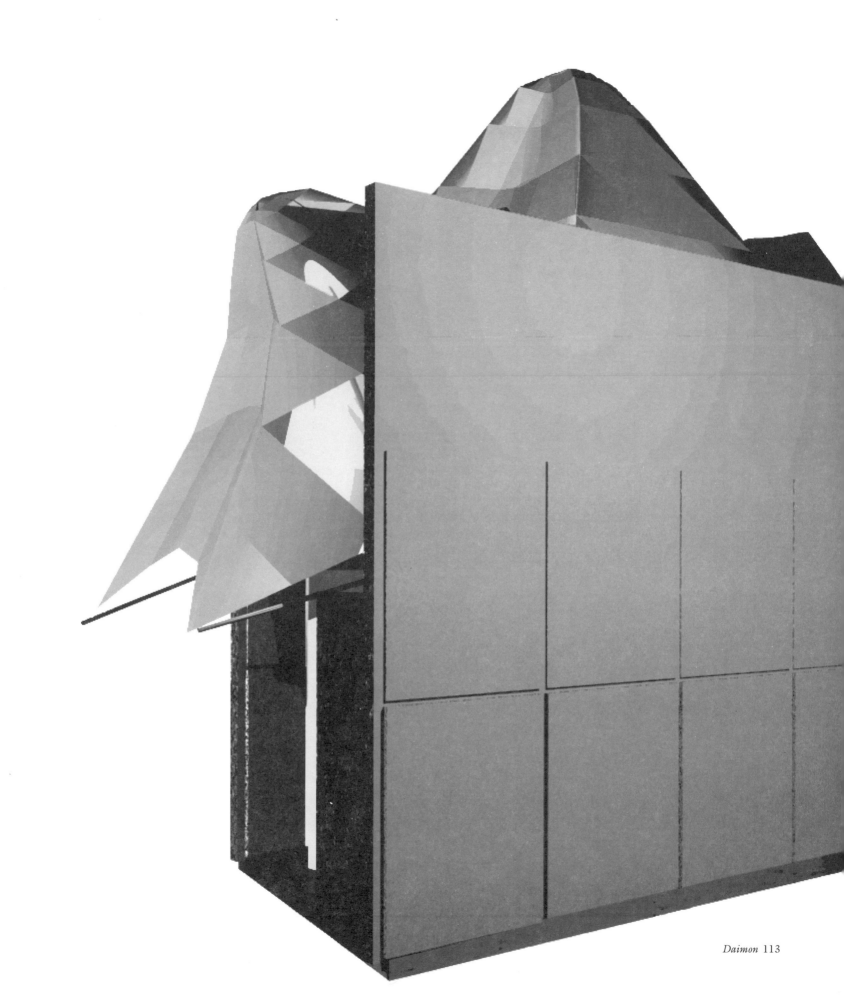

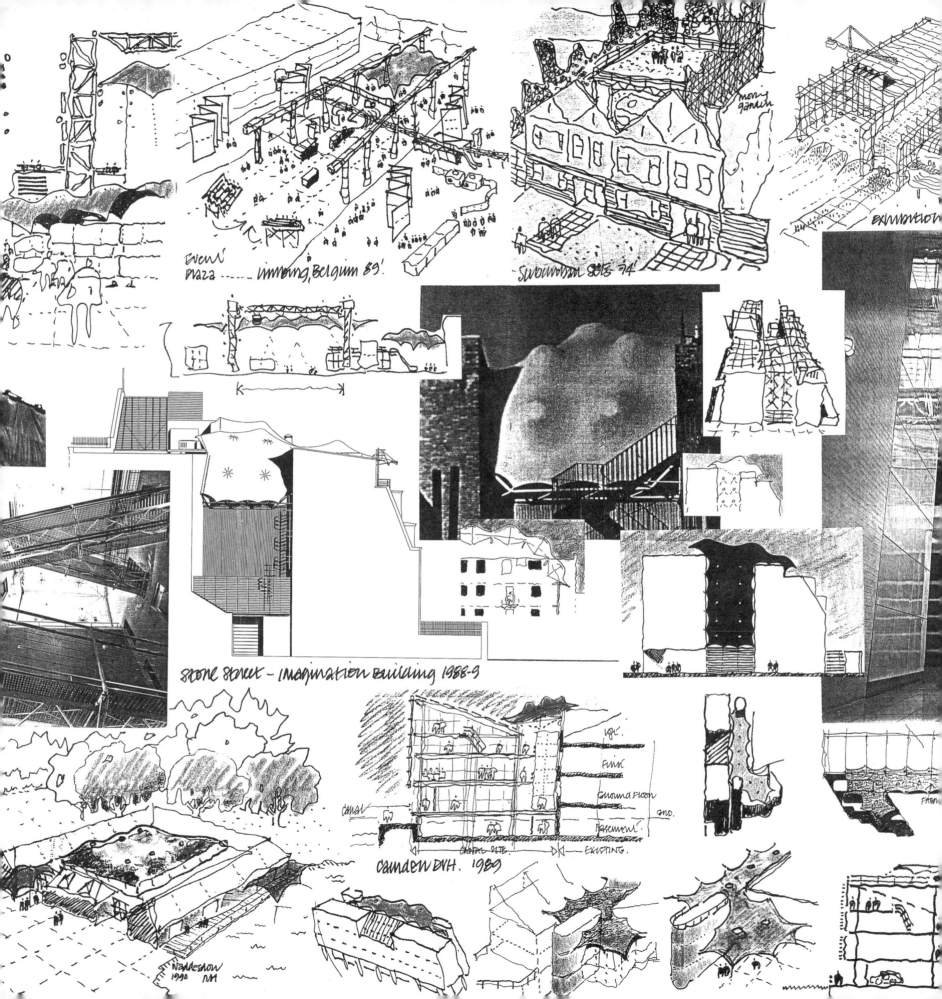

Event
Plaza ----- Limburg, Belgium 89'

Suburban Sols 74'

EXHIBITION

Stone Street - Imagination Building 1988-9

Light
Fund
Ground Floor
and.
Basement
Canal
Camal Site Existing.

Camden DVH. 1989

Nalderslow
1990
MM

988
travel

stair lifts
DEPOT
stair/lifts
semi-permanent exhib
clip-on toilets etc
crane zone
CHANGING EXHIB
PLANT - TOILETS.
crane
PERMANENT EXHIB. THEATRE etc
stair lifts
stair lifts
Facade
STREET.
26M

STREET.

Autumn looking West.

Imagination Bldg
Stude II.

Imagination Bldg
Stude II.
3·12·87.

Infotainment Project 92'

crane.

Daimon

One of Ron Herron's long-standing preoccupations has been to do with the slot: the problem of inserting a function into an existing town or city setting. It is something architects deal with all the time in the city: a tall, narrow, deep space flanked on either side by adjoining blank walls.

The Daimon site wasn't quite like that. It had traditional-style Japanese town houses on either side. So what the Herrons did was to create the archetypal slot by building the necessary flanking walls which serve only up to a point as external side elevations. In a sense they redefined the site conditions in order to get on with thinking about the possibilities of this particular slot: wrapping, insertions, sets, and, perhaps because people would wait there for the once-hourly bus, transience.

Herron's design for the Imagination Building had been based on the same kind of thinking. It was actually an elongated extruded H form (two parallel buildings joined by a crossbar of lavatories and service spaces): he immediately grasped that here was a slot which could be wrapped and into which a whole range of things could potentially be inserted, among them, at one stage of the design, a multi-storey animated multimedia robot.

The thinking around Daimon is inherent in a number of projects of the late 1980s in which Herron created the slot by building support structures either side of big spaces. Into these could be inserted normally temporary architectural and technological elements. The lineage of this idea has some of its roots in his collection of <u>Sets</u> of the 1970s. The notion behind this series of designs was that the primary functions of the street façade (especially in a suburban Britain where the conservative anti-architecture planning system reigns implacably supreme) were not architecturally important. Their function was really to express the occupier's self-image. The architectural task was in devising what was inserted behind the stage-set-like façade in the long, narrow-gutted plot of the typical suburban site.

At the Imagination Building the original intention was to leave the walls as they found them. When the exposed walls turned out to be unpleasantly patchy, Herron did the minimum necessary: he simply painted them white. The fabric roof was the simplest and cheapest expedient solution. While it had a guaranteed 15-year minimum life (around the same as a conventional industrial roof), it looked transitory. Together with the walls, it implied impermanence and encouraged its users to treat it as a working, un-sacrosanct environment. However visually stunning as a space in real life, its unheroic materials and roof structure were in a sense an incitement for its users to create <u>ad hoc</u> temporary installations, insertions, performances, events. Which is precisely what has happened since it opened.

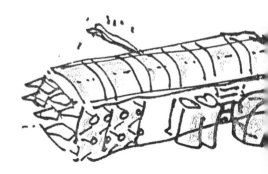

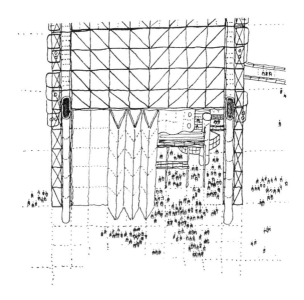

Herron points out that, although most of his designs are predicated on distinctive lightweight structures, he is not particularly preoccupied by the engineering end. His argument is that we are no longer in the age of heroic engineering. This is the era of the black box, '… which physically is not much of an architectural device. In our period architectural problems don't have that heroic manifestation. In the end you can only draw the event.'

As Andrew Herron points out, the drawings are really about the event possibilities. If he could, Ron Herron would use such technology as holography to create spaces, air curtains to keep out the elements. He argues, 'Of course we are always interested in the idea of the enclosure – but even that could be created by some invisible device. What you happen to be sitting on is not in the end all that interesting. What is interesting is change. You are really dealing only with the space and with the event.'

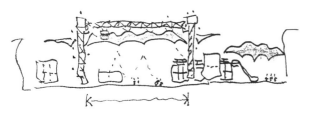

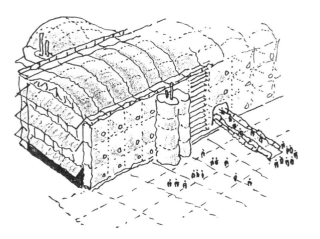

Project details

Kurobe
Client: Kurobe City Council with Urban Factory
Design team: Ron Herron, Andrew Herron, James Phillips
Contract value: ¥4.2 million
Engineering and fabrication: Taiyo Corporation
Local architect: Kazuo Igarashi
Practice name: Toyama Kenchiku Kenkyu Jo
Completion: February 1993

Kosugi
Client: Kosugi City Council with Urban Factory
Design team: Ron Herron, Andrew Herron, James Phillips
Contract value: ¥5.2 million
Engineering and fabrication: Taiyo Corporation
Local architects: Yazuhiro Fukumi and Shigeaki Doda
Practice name: Fukumi Sekkei
Completion: August 1992

Daimon
Client: Daimon City Council with Urban Factory
Design team: Ron Herron, James Phillips, Simon Herron
Contract value: ¥4.2 million
Engineering and fabrication: Taiyo Corporation
Local architect: Shigeo Yoshida
Practice name: Yoshida Kenchiku Jimsho
Completion: (projected) May 1993

The computer models were constructed by:
Andrew Herron, Anthony Leung, A. A. Nik, and
Towon Sin Gan